"I have been deeply moved by the meaning Jennifer gives to what I thought were my everyday experiences and it is my belief that though the primary audience of this book may be girls on the spectrum, others will find great value in the words, findings, and experiences of the vibrant Jennifer Cook O'Toole. Because no matter if we fall within the spectrum, are navigating the cusp, or we find ourselves elsewhere, aren't we all wired just a little bit differently?"

— *Amy Serrano*, Glamour *magazine's "Woman of the Year,"*
Internationally-Celebrated Filmmaker, Writer and Humanitarian

"I picked up this book, and could literally not put it down until I had read it through. As a developmental pediatrician, I frequently identify children with autism and address their needs. I am relieved to find such an engaging resource specifically geared towards the population of girls becoming women. Jennifer Cook O'Toole has created a witty, insightful, and memorable guide to the workings of the young female mind. No clinician, parent, or young woman affected by autism should be without this book."

— *Wendy J. Ross, MD, CNN Hero, FAAP Director, Center for*
Pediatric Development, and Founder, Autism Inclusion Resources

"As a psychologist specializing in working with females with ASD, I am truly privileged to see sparks of great beauty daily; the girls and young women I meet and work with amaze me with their caring, their talents, and their resilience. And yet too often they do not see it themselves. O'Toole's *Sisterhood* is an 'at last' gift I can return to them—a safe invitation for every young woman to read and journey through while getting to know herself. For any girl on the spectrum who has felt alone, like she is the only one, *Sisterhood* is a chance for her to crack open her heart and let a small voice whisper—'that's like me.' Thank you, thank you Jennifer a thousand times over for this beautiful bursting book that I cannot wait to share!"

— *Shana Nichols, Ph.D., Licensed Psychologist, Owner, Director*
and Researcher, ASPIRE Center for Learning and Development

"*Sisterhood of the Spectrum* is a smart, cheeky, authentically unique read for ALL girls. Just like she does in her other Asperkids books, Jennifer entertains and inspires and makes the reader feel as if she is talking just to them…because she is! The numerous empowering messages throughout the book such as, 'A candle doesn't lose its flame when it lights another candle' leave the reader feeling heard and remind all woman that we matter and are perfect just the way we are! If you have a tween/teen or young adult daughter, granddaughter, sister, or friend you will want them to read this book."

—Zoom Autism *magazine*

"*Sisterhood of the Spectrum* is over-the-top awesome in every way. There were times it actually made me cry with its dead-on description of the truth. Simply by inviting spectrum girls to connect with their own sisterhood, it makes a huge contribution, and that's just the beginning. With humor, directness, wisdom and honesty, this book packs spectrum girls' tool kits with what they need to grow and thrive while discovering their true selves. I couldn't put it down and can't wait to buy it for myself and share it with every clinician and every family and every girl I know who's part of this powerful and gifted community. As a psychologist with the honor and privilege of working with Aspie girls, I am deeply grateful to Jennifer Cook O'Toole for this treasure of a guidebook."

—*Carol Moog, Ph.D., co-author of* The Autism Playbook for Teens, *psychologist, The Miquon School and in private practice*

Sisterhood of the Spectrum

by the same author

The Asperkid's (Secret) Book of Social Rules
**The Handbook of Not-So-Obvious Social Guidelines
for Tweens and Teens with Asperger Syndrome**
Jennifer Cook O'Toole
Illustrated by Brian Bojanowski
ISBN 978 1 84905 915 2
eISBN 978 0 85700 685 1

Asperkids
**An Insider's Guide to Loving, Understanding and
Teaching Children with Asperger Syndrome**
Jennifer Cook O'Toole
Foreword by Liane Holliday Willey
ISBN 978 1 84905 902 2
eISBN 978 0 85700 647 9

The Asperkid's Launch Pad
Home Design to Empower Everyday Superheroes
Jennifer Cook O'Toole
ISBN 978 1 84905 931 2
eISBN 978 0 85700 727 8

The Asperkid's Game Plan
Extraordinary Minds, Purposeful Play... Ordinary Stuff
Jennifer Cook O'Toole
ISBN 978 1 84905 959 6
eISBN 978 0 85700 779 7

The Asperkid's Not-Your-Average-Coloring-Book
Jennifer Cook O'Toole
ISBN 978 1 84905 958 9

Sisterhood
of the Spectrum

An Asperger Chick's Guide to Life

Jennifer Cook O'Toole

Illustrated by Anne-Louise Richards

Jessica Kingsley *Publishers*
London and Philadelphia

First published in 2015
by Jessica Kingsley Publishers
73 Collier Street
London N1 9BE, UK
and
400 Market Street, Suite 400
Philadelphia, PA 19106, USA

www.jkp.com

Library of Congress Cataloging in Publication Data
O'Toole, Jennifer Cook.
Sisterhood of the spectrum : an Asperger chick's guide to life / Jennifer Cook
O'Toole ; illustrated by
Anne-Louise Richards.
pages cm
ISBN 978-1-84905-790-5 (alk. paper)
1. Asperger's syndrome in adolescence. 2. Teenage girls--Life skills guides. 3.
Teenagers with
disabilities--Life skills guides. I. Title.
RJ506.A9O864 2015
616.85'883200835--dc23
2014047759

British Library Cataloguing in Publication Data
A CIP catalogue record for this book is available from the British Library

ISBN 978 1 84905 790 5
eISBN 978 1 78450 056 6

Printed and bound in the United States

MIX
Paper from
responsible sources
FSC
www.fsc.org FSC® C013483

"And though she be but little,
she is fierce."

—*William Shakespeare*

"It's risky," said pride.
"It's impossible," said experience.
"It's nonsensical," said reason.
"Try anyway," whispered the heart.
"I want to see you be brave."

—*Jennifer Cook O'Toole*

For ALL the beautiful girls
who refuse to talk about rather than talk to…
who know that being "feminine" means owning and
enjoying your body
with confidence…
who glean wit from our foremothers
and shower love generously on all who come next…
who build each other up instead of tearing each other
down and
never have to begin a sentence with,
"I don't want to sound like a mean girl, but…"

For the mighty beauties of all ages—
You are equally breathtaking all made up
and completely stripped down.

Thank you for giving me a space in your hearts.

And especially for my Maura Ann…
the anything-but-typical girl at the center of my world.
I am SO lucky to get to love you.
"Because I knew you…I have been changed. For good."

Acknowledgments

With great thanks...to the GIRLS.

To Anne-Louise Richards for your spectacular artistic talent, wickedly delicious wit, and most of all...for saying that you see yourself in me. I am humbled to get to be a part of your FANTASTIC journey.

To Rene Katkowski for being the Zen to my chaotic whirlygig. Thank you for every effort, every email, every text, every brainwave you've put into making this book happen. May I do Sera proud—because you certainly have.

To my mom, Jane Cook, for being such an inspiration in more ways than I'll ever be able to say. I love you, Mommy.

To my Spectrum Sisters who've contributed their wisdom to this book. I am simply blown away that I even get to know you. You honor me with your participation in this adventure.

To 11-year-old Beth Paine, who asked, "How soon will this book be out?" And who, when I answered, "Soon, I hope," grinned from ear to ear and shouted, "YES!". Everyone needs a friend like you, Beth.

And to my daughter, Maura Ann, for making me want to write this book in the first place. I love you too big for words, Munchkin.

Contents

A Beautiful Idea 13

This Calls for a Rewrite 17

The Microphone: Let Me Hear Your Voice, Spectrum Girls 19

Seeing You. 35

Quotealicious. **39**

1. Spelunking: Discovering the Typical
    Diamond You Already Are 40

2. Follow the Yellow Brick Road: Why You Don't Need a
    GPS to "Find Yourself". 44

3. No Spoilers, Sweetie: A Story About Stories
    …and a Relay Race. 53

4. Let Me Introduce You…to Yourself. 60

5. Playing Dominoes in Reverse: Know Where You Want to
    Go if You Want to Get There 69

6. Decisions, Decisions: What You Choose
    Is What Continues. 78

7. "No" Is a Complete Sentence: People Pleasing vs.
    Pleasing Yourself. 84

8. Anxiety: The Nemesis of All Awesomeness. 92

    Something Special: The Box on the Shelf. 104

9. You Cannot Actually Die of Embarrassment. 106

10. Blanching at Perfectionism: Real Girls Aren't Perfect. And
    Perfect Girls Aren't Real. 112

    Special Stuff: Daisy's Lesson 125

Quotealicious. **127**

11. Sexuality: The Venn Diagram They
    Didn't Teach in School 128

12. No "Right" Way to "Be a Girl" 134

13. The Question Box: Why THAT Would Be a Good Idea
    (or Not) 143

14. Body Blow: How You "Measure Up" 153

15. Function Over Form: Your Shape, Senses…and Bras 160

16. Why *Romeo and Juliet* Is Not a Love Story 169

17. Danger Signs 178

18. The Particulars: Falling in Like with Your
    Eyes Wide Open 188

    Quotealicious 196

    Something Special: The Evil Twins 197

19. "Ain't I a Woman?": Girl Power. For All 200

20. Bullies, Mean Girls, and Stuff That Actually Works 207

    Need to Know (and Believe) Bulletpoint Recap 227

    Your Song 234

    RESOURCES: PLEASE TRUST THEM. PLEASE USE THEM 237

A Beautiful Idea

So, I have this idea.
And I was hoping you'd maybe give it a listen.
Ready?

My idea is that people need to say—out loud
the nice things they usually just think
and keep to themselves.

Like, "Your laugh is awesome. It's all bright and shiny and
    wonderful."
Or, "I love your wild imagination…you make everything more
    fun."
Or, "It's nice being quiet with you."
All those real bits that slip by.
Big things. Little things. All of it. It matters. Because *you* matter.
For real.

I don't know why people don't do that more often.
Especially girls.
A candle doesn't lose its fire
when it lights another candle.
Same thing goes for us.
Telling you the honest, wonderful things I see in you
doesn't mean I'm less. And it doesn't mean I'm more.
My success isn't your failure. And yours isn't mine.
There's plenty of good to go around.
So, I thought I'd tell you about *you*.
Because…you're kind of amazing
in a lot of ways.
And maybe you don't see what I see.

I'm not talking about big, flashy stuff…although that's great, too.
I'm talking about the little ways you crack open your heart—
even when you're scared and other people don't understand
    why…
Because when you're vulnerable like that, joy sneaks in…and you
    light up.

I'm talking about your mind.
I love how your whirring, busy brain is always curious.
Always wondering. And asking.
Always learning.
And then imagining.
Because that's how you'll change the world.

I'm talking about your kindness. The way
your heart hurts—
really hurts—
when the world is cruel to other
people or creatures.
Because I've noticed that the kindest hearts are often the ones
that have been hurt the most.
And the way you turn pain into love without even thinking
takes my breath away.

I'm talking about how everyone tells you just to be yourself—
then adds, "…only not like that."
And I say, "Yes. Do it JUST like that."

I'm talking about how maybe being opinionated and strong and
bossy isn't bad.
Maybe it just *sounds* nicer to say
passionate
and determined
and ambitious
and driven…
But they end up being pretty much the same thing.
And you're passionate and determined and ambitious and driven
about the things you love.
And it's amazing to watch.

I'm talking about being beautiful.
But I'm not talking about a "thigh gap"
or straight teeth
or jean size.
I'm talking about being beautiful because you are
mighty
and sassy
and gentle
and valuable

in ways that have nothing to do with whether someone else
    includes you
or picks you
or even likes you.

And you're already beautiful. Now.
You're beautiful in the way your voice changes when you talk
    about something you love.
You're beautiful in the way your eyes crinkle when you look up at
    the sky and feel small.
You're beautiful in those secret tears you cry when you think
    you're a mistake instead of realizing you're a miracle.
You're beautiful in the way you fight and argue and refuse to give
    up on what you believe.
You're beautiful in *every* way that you are *not* typical.

Yes. You're beautiful, alright.

You're the kind of beautiful that only gets bigger and better with
    time…
A work in progress.
Undiluted you-ness.
And even if you can't see it yet,
that's OK.
I do.
And you will.
And together, we'll make the world a more beautiful place
    to be us.

This Calls for a Rewrite

Everyone operates based on assumptions. Everyone. How you interpret my phrasing. How I read your body language. No person is a *tabula rasa* (a blank slate). Which means that no matter how well you think you understand someone else—or yourself—any time you feel confused, there's a good chance that assumptions and misunderstandings are to blame.

Why? In a lot of ways, we each live in our own little worlds— and we like those little worlds. But if we're going to connect with others in the *real* world, the trick is to stop arguing about whose "miniverse" is right and whose is wrong. Instead, we have to readjust our focus and learn to experience life together—as "and" instead of "but."

That's harder than it seems. Every day, we hear old tapes playing in new situations instead of listening to what's actually being said. We over-rely on past experiences and limited frames of reference to interpret entirely new events and people. We filter others' words and actions, and then recalibrate them within our own minds to jive with what's more familiar, logical, or understandable. That means that much of our understanding—of ourselves, of people we know casually, and of the people we love deeply—is distorted. On most days, in most ways, most of us are loving, despising, dismissing, and reacting to "facts" and folks that are almost entirely fictional. That's not a story with a happy ending. But *you* are.

So you know what? This whole "figuring yourself out" thing? Yeah. This calls for a serious rewrite.

The Microphone

Let Me Hear Your Voice, Spectrum Girls

Not every girl can say that one of her life's most revealing moments involves a pink feather boa and a dangling microphone. Then again, I'm not every girl (and neither are you). But the feathers and microphone thing? Yep. That's all me.

Alright. Let me try to set the scene for you. Imagine a dark high school auditorium, every one of those flip-up seats filled. The air is humid, maybe a little dank. The school orchestra is playing a show tune at full volume. And through colored films, a single, white spotlight directs all eight hundred pairs of eyes to one person: me.

Center stage. All alone. I was fifteen, dressed up as someone completely opposite from the girl my classmates (thought they) knew. That night, I'd be the star of the show. The heartbreaker. Literally. I was Lola, of "Whatever Lola Wants (Lola gets)." Black satin slip dress. Flowing red hair. Black fishnets and heels. And although I was in costume in many ways, I'd never felt more... well, more *me*.

The music was electric, and every move was right. Until the railing. But we'll get to that soon.

Often, life's biggest events happen without any warning. There you are, doing whatever you've planned—stopping for a latte, studying for an exam, starting a new job—then...BAM! You meet the girl who'll be your best friend for the next twenty years. You get the news that someone you love is really ill. Your parents announce the family will be moving. You have an unexpected conversation that leads to unexpected love. Those sorts of things aren't in your daily planner. They just happen. Suddenly, in the blink of an eye, the whole world seems to shift. Gravity loses hold on you. And everything turns upside down.

Other times, well, you can pretty much guarantee that the day will be special. Graduations. A big game. Special trips. Birthdays. Sometimes things turn out as expected, sometimes not. Either way, you know from the get-go that the day isn't going to be run-of-the-mill.

But the most game-changing events—the ones where you really find out who you are, what you're made of, how much you'll take, whom you'll defend, what you'll (actually) try even if you never knew you had the courage to do it—well, those events are a mix. You know something is ahead...you just can't say how you'll act in the moment or how life will change after the fact.

That March evening in the spotlight was one of *those* defining moments. More than just my first solo in the first performance of a small-town school show, that night was a proving ground. In front of a sold-out crowd, I was either going to break out of the social pigeonhole I'd been forced into for ten years or be such a poor excuse for "the most beautiful woman on the planet" that escaping from a New Jersey suburb to the Australian outback might seem like a completely rational move.

You know, looking back, I'm not really sure if I was unbelievably brave or just incredibly naive. Probably, it was a mix of the two. What I do know for sure is that as I crossed that stage, every step was perfect, every note true—and every person in the crowd was hypnotized. In adolescent-Cinderella style, my entire world was changing. Well, sort of.

When I'm Talking About Me…I'm Not, Really

Before we go on, I have to make something clear: you've been reading about me—and at some points in this book, you will again. That's because it only seems fair that if you're going to be kind enough to listen to my ideas, you deserve to know that I'm talking from personal experience—not from what I learned in a class or a job. Nope. This is wisdom (and heartache and mess-ups and discoveries) in the first person.

Next question: Why should you care what has happened to me (some stranger)? Simple. The truth is, the stories you're reading aren't entirely about me. In who's and where's and when's, yes, of course, they're mine. But in much bigger, more important ways, they're about us. We're different people, you and me. We're different ages, and maybe even from different countries. The particulars of my life and of yours can't be identical. I mean, they don't have to be.

Maybe I'm talkative and you're quiet. Maybe you'd rather hang upside down from a tree than be caught dead in lipstick. Maybe I'm in Ravenclaw (I totally am) and you couldn't possibly be less interested in *Harry Potter*. But those are just surface details. As girls on the spectrum, our brains function differently than most, but in very important ways, they are wired similarly to one another. That's why we share such "down deep" basics. We just come with intense feelings, deep loyalty, a strong sense of justice, compassion for those who are left out or left behind, and confusion about how it is we can mean well but misunderstand so often.

So here's the truth: a lot of what I'm going to tell you about *me* is actually about some of the most important parts of *you*. Why? **Because you may not be typical, but, around me, you are extremely NORMAL.**

As I was saying…attention of one kind or another has pretty much followed me since I showed up on this planet. Just imagine a hospital nursery full of tightly swaddled newborn babies—a sea of pink and blue (and red…that'd be me, the ginger-fuzzed one). When you're born a redhead (or an Aspie), "blending" is pretty much impossible. You can't help but stick out at least a bit. It's just something you have to learn to go with.

And I went with it. At two, I remember seeing a *Sesame Street* episode where Big Bird was watching some ballerinas perform *Swan Lake*. "Do you like the pretty dancing, Jenny?" my mom asked in that sing-song voice adults use on kids. "Yes," I answered, completely matter-of-factly. "I can do that." Of course, my mom thought I was just being cute, but she went ahead and obliged, signing me up for dancing school. The thing was, I hadn't meant to be cute. I'd been serious. And it turned out I was right.

From the start, the teachers were floored—and there they put me, the little redhead, center stage. Adorable. Precocious. Three different times, talent agents approached my parents. "She's perfect for television!" they said. And soon enough, I was chewing Wonder Bread for the camera. I read and spoke like a little adult. The natural teacher's pet. All eyes this way. Applause and smiles. For a while, anyway.

Secret Stars: Attention, Approval… and the Vast Wasteland In-Between

Behind closed doors, even the quietest, most introverted girl has moments when she transforms into a secret star. The center of attention. Confident. Bold. Full of life. You know what I mean. With music blaring, you may belt a tune into a hairbrush handle or strut your stuff down a runway that is, in fact, your bedroom. You wave to the adoring crowd, everyone wildly cheering your big-screen debut. You smile just right into the mirror and tell (yourself) the funniest joke. Suddenly, lunchtime is never awkward again, you're picked for every team, and fights break out over who can be your lab partner...

In those private times, more than just being accepted, you are perfection. More than being "OK," you are grand. In those fantastical moments, you get to be celebrated, admired, and adored. You are—finally—what everyone else wants to be, instead of the other way around.

But the prize we're all craving isn't *really* attention. It's approval. And it turns out that attention and approval are not even close to the same thing. Now, I've already explained that adult attention came easily without my really trying. What I've left out is this: I also got a lot of attention from kids—only for the most part, it was *not* the kind of attention you'd want.

Who Am I?

When I was a little girl, I asked my mother this question: "Who am I?"

"What do you mean, who *are* you?" she replied shortly, her back turned to me. "You're Jenny." I sighed. Yeah, mom. Thanks. That much I had. As usual, what I meant didn't, apparently, match up with what I was actually saying. My chest tightened; my small brow furrowed in frustration. "No, Mom. What I mean is, who is *me*?" I pressed, straining to explain. "If I can say '*my* brain,' then my brain isn't me, it's something that *belongs* to me. And that'd be the same for '*my* spirit' and '*my*self.' You see? So, who is the *me* behind the '*my*'?" How could something be so clear in *my* mind yet utterly confuse everyone else around me? My mind, then *and* now, always felt transparent—every thought obvious—clearly visible to everyone. And, logic followed, if those ideas and feelings and fears and questions were as obvious as I *knew* them to be, yet were ignored (or more often, scoffed at), then the only really "obvious" fact was this: I wasn't worth answering. Understanding me was a bother. Connecting with me was unnecessary. Or boring. Or uncomfortable. Which meant that I, too, was boring, weird, and unnecessary. That's what I believed…and that's what life continued to teach.

On that particular day, my little-kid brain was in overdrive—stuck, wheels spinning, engine revving—without anyone "getting" my question. Without anyone getting *me*. I didn't *want* an answer. I *needed* an answer. Because, I suppose, I needed to know I was worth the effort.

Maybe it was about this time that my mother got a glimpse into what lay ahead of her: questions. Endless questions and ceaseless analyzing. Boundless oceans of information. An insatiable thirst to know and super-intense (entirely sincere) feelings. Life with the volume turned way up. The truth is, my perpetual crush of ideas and words tired my mom. They've tired a lot of people over the years—and, I suppose, occasionally entranced a few. "You think too much," she said, shaking her head, befuddled. "I've never thought that much about anything." But I had no idea how to be anything else. I still don't. And back then, I figured, I could just ask the right question at the right time of the right person, or move the right way to the right music, or wear the right costume…then maybe—just maybe—I could learn how to feel the one thing I'd never managed to be with much success: maybe I could finally learn how to feel lovable.

Game's Locked

By age six, I was used to being "locked" out of playground games and running the few blocks home after school. Matthew, who was three years older than me, followed me every day. And even now, decades later, I can hear his voice shouting from about two house-lengths behind, "Hey, Dictionary Brain! You know nobody likes you, right? You know everybody hates you? Hey! Encyclopedia Head! Are you listening to me?" I'd try to ignore him. I'd try to pick up the pace. I'd try to talk over him to the younger girl by my side, humiliated that even a "little kid" knew my shame.

"I heard you go home for lunch, Dictionary Brain. Is that because no one will sit with you in the cafeteria?!" Yes, it was. Even in the cold winter air, my cheeks burned hot. And when, one afternoon, I realized I'd dropped a mitten along the way—a loss that was sure to make my mom mad—I wouldn't turn back for it. No, I wouldn't turn back for anything.

I'm not sure why Matthew had such a problem with me. Of course, as an adult, I'll sagely opine that it had more to do with his own unhappiness than with me at all. And maybe that's partially true. But the whole story was bigger. It usually is.

In my little town at my little school, teachers had freedom that modern teachers don't. They knew I was bored in class, so they'd let me go—alone—to the school library…for hours. What a gift. I'd just walk in, wave at the always-glad-to-see-me librarian, choose a new shelf, and start reading. One by one, I'd savor each book, exploring long-lost worlds, imagining myself happily entrenched in the time or place—any other time or place—to which I so obviously belonged. To me, the biography section was a wall full of friends. The dinosaur shelves were my own personal Jurassic Park. And the made-up stories were wonderful, too. Rich tales—the stuff of fantastic, time-traveling adventures—gave me the chance to "try on" feelings that real life didn't. I could be necessary, silly, maybe even liked. Dewy Decimal (the library classification system) was, in a way, my guide to a destination where people made sense… and so did I. The only "fee" for endless time among the stacks? I had to write extra book reports every now and then. Big deal. As far as I was concerned, I'd scored a major coup.

The teachers thought it a good plan, too. In fact, my report on Christopher Columbus so impressed them that I was invited, as a second grader, to read the whole thing aloud to the fifth-grade classes as an example of how to write an "excellent paper." One of those fifth graders just happened to be Matthew. And, it turned out, Matthew was neither a strong reader nor a strong writer. So when a certain seven-year-old redhead waltzed into his classroom to "teach" him, he probably felt embarrassed and stupid. Though it wasn't my idea, I was certainly proud of that invitation. By extension, it's not hard to see how chin-up, clear-voiced, "Dictionary Brain" Jenny became the embodiment of everything that little boy despised in himself.

It's not hard to see *now*, but I didn't see anything then—or for many more years afterwards. It took decades and a strangely named diagnosis for me to understand that my hurt came both from without (I mean really, what teacher thought *that* situation was a good idea?!) and from within. Arrogance and insecurity are two sides of the same coin. The greater one grows, the bolder the other becomes in compensation. In other words, if there was nothing else I could do right, then couldn't school be my "specialty?" The adults sure liked me for it! Why, then, didn't the kids? It never occurred to me—not for a moment—that in trying to sound confident, I sounded horribly arrogant. In trying to be helpful, I sounded parental. In trying to make friends, I made a fool of myself. Over and over again.

Brain Power...and Hush-Your-Brain Power

Fast forward back to that auditorium. All eyes on me. I'd danced since I was two. I'd read countless poems and stories to school audiences. I'd done this performing thing before. But never like this—never in a way that was entirely UN-academic. That night, I was singing my lungs out, whole-heartedly declaring to the entire student body (and anybody else who happened to waltz through those doors) that I was much more than a Dictionary Brain. That I could be fun and funny and jaw-dropping, too. That I deserved to be wanted, not just endured. And they were listening.

Then I got to the railing.

During the next sequence of the dance, I was going to have to continue to sing while bending waaaaay back over the banister at the top of the stairs that led down from the stage. The choreography had me doing the dip and wiggling the boa, then slinking down the steps and into the crowd, where I would have to continue to sing and interact with audience members. But suddenly, while blinded by the spotlight in the dark auditorium in front of eight hundred people, there was a problem: I straightened up from the rail and felt an odd pop in the small of my back, then a sudden catch. Something was yanking off my dress!

Just one covert glance and I knew what had happened: Before showtime, the battery portion of my wireless microphone was hooked onto the waistband at the top of those oh-so-glamorous fishnet stockings. Somehow, in the process of leaning backwards, the handrail had managed to knock the battery pack loose, and now the entire (really heavy) thing was dangling between my legs while pulling down the front of the dress where the mic was actually clipped. Oh yes, and I was still singing and—in a quick mental check—realized that I had only a few measures left to twirl that boa before I was supposed to be shimmying down the steps.

There was no time to think. There was only time to act. And that, probably, was what saved me.

Many things that seem perfectly clear to typical girls couldn't be more confusing for us. Friendships. Fashion. Facebook. We don't just "pick those things up" without effort. Instead, we have to figure them out. Observing, analyzing patterns, gleaning information from everything and everyone we can. Our minds can be our greatest asset—and toughest enemy. Without meaning to, we anxiously overthink some things and impulsively under-think others. What we almost never do, though, is to listen to our instincts (let alone trust them). Except when life comes at you really fast, there isn't always time to think. There's just time to do. Sometimes, that can be a really, really good thing. You have no chance to overthink. All you can do is keep moving.

So what did I do? I bent at the knees, did a sly, winky peek-a-boo through the bars of the railing and snatched the battery pack without anyone seeing. There was a hitch in my voice, yes, but video playbacks barely recorded a hiccup. I spun those feathers. I sang my song. And I kept going.

Years later, when my school guidance counselor recommended me to an elite university, he didn't write about my grades. He didn't write about my extracurricular activities or my civic leadership. Instead, he wrote, "For many years now, I've put forth candidates for admission to your school. Each one was brilliant. Each one was a standout. So I never understood why each one was, in turn, rejected. That is, I didn't understand until I met Jenny." And he went on to tell the story of the fishnets and the microphone.

Everything in that moment had spelled disaster, he said. Every insecurity and fear should've been triggered. Instead, I'd taken one (secret) breath to steady myself and never stopped moving. It was, he wrote, remarkable—part of some edge, some depth to everything I felt and said and did. Survival. Resilience. Beauty.

The magic came, he said, from some unnamed, extraordinary combination of complexities, of distractions and focus. But I *can* name it. Now. **It's a difference, alright, but not one unique to me. It's a difference unique to us. And it's called Asperger syndrome (or autism, or AS).** Pick a label. Grab a thesaurus. It doesn't really matter which words you choose.

Labelish

A "label" doesn't make anyone an "Aspie" or "autistic" any more than declaring, "It's a girl!" caused you to be female. I was diagnosed—or let's say "identified" if it feels less disease-ish— three years ago. Was that the first time I felt "different?" Hardly. Think back to the library bookshelves. Think back to my Columbus report.

And think back to the auditorium. The neurological hardwiring that makes me blind to social self-sabotage is the same which tells me that actions speak louder than words. That resilience trumps precision. That bravery isn't something you plan for. That wonder and possibility and wild imagination are truer and more beautiful than anything I know.

Quirks, misunderstandings, hurts, and blunders, as well as courage, tenacity, fidelity, and joy, are all part of being the kind of different we are. Even in a world that's coming to understand autism/Asperger's a bit more, spectrum girls are amazingly invisible—even to ourselves. Which is ridiculous because we're everywhere. We always have been. This world is as much ours as anyone else's. More than that, this world *needs* our intensity, our wit, our creativity, our work, our ideas, our kindness…it needs *us*. Really. It needs *you*.

Keep calm and carry on? No thanks. I'd rather stir it up and change the world. And I need you by my side, doing and being—not doubting and overthinking. So that, dear girls, is why I've written this book. Because you deserve to look in the mirror and see far more than a face or body part…more than someone's daughter or student or sister or girlfriend.

> You are your own wondrous occasion.
> More than a one-in-a-million kind of girl,
> you're a once-in-a-lifetime kind of person.
> You're mighty.
> And beautiful.
> And brilliant.

Girls Are No "Less Aspie." We're Just Less Obvious.

Maybe you've never quite "blended" with other people, or you've had to work really hard at it. But you don't really see yourself in any of the things you've heard about autism or Asperger's, either. Sort of like being invisible to everyone.

Well, it turns out there's a reason we often don't recognize ourselves here *or* there. When doctors, parents, teachers, therapists, and even television describe "typical" spectrum kids, without meaning to, they're describing typically "male" spectrum traits—patterns first noticed by observing boys. Only boys. And we aren't boys.

So they miss and mislabel us. They let us down. Often.

You may know that Thomas the Train, dinosaurs, space, architecture, and transportation are very common special interests for spectrum boys. Now, I definitely loved dinos and space…but the rest of those? Nah, not really. Maybe you loved airplanes. Maybe not. The point is that a lot of girls also geek out over dog breeds, horses, cute collectibles like Ever After High, Littlest Pet Shop, My Little Ponies, or Smurfs. Girls love our sci-fi, too, but we'd just as soon dive into biographies, family trees of kings and queens, Broadway shows, or historical clothing. Maybe, instead of Pokemon, our love is fairies or Barbies, especially if those Barbies are quietly acting out a historical event or favorite Greek myth. And don't be surprised if, when we play "princess," we're *not* Cinderella. We're being Juliet.

Our Story (AKA What This Book Is NOT)

What's it like to be a girl on the spectrum? That's a question I get a lot, and although it's taken me awhile to come up with a decent answer, I think this may finally be it: too much. **We feel too much. React too much. Say too much. Need too much. So says the world. Except the world is wrong.**

Somewhere along my way, I discovered that **there is no way to be too you**. Ask someone to behave as or aspire to anything less, and you are asking that someone to *be* something less.

And you know what's most ironic? The word "autism" comes from the same root as "*auto*graph" and "*auto*mobile." "Auto" means "self." We *are* self-referenced, certainly. **We have a hard time separating our wants and desires and thoughts from everyone else's, true. But that's not because we have so much self. It's because we have so little.**

Girls, I know what it's like to be a teen—a young woman— growing up certain of some talents, and equally certain that I'd be called out as a "fraud" at any moment. I know what it's like to be outside of the "bell curve" because I am a woman on the spectrum, raising a daughter on the spectrum. I know what it is to hate myself. To fake it. To gauge my worth by other people's say-so.

From the time I was in elementary school, I began thinking about—analyzing, studying—what it meant to be a "successful" woman. I read and thought. And then read and thought some more. I read lots of biographies. I studied fashion. And you know what all that studying got me? Confused.

The instructions I was getting were mixed. They still are. Be "this" not "that" (except for sometimes *do* be "that"—just don't be too obvious about it).

Magazines tell you how you're supposed to look. Movies tell you what you're supposed to say. Teachers and parents and "experts" tell you how you're supposed to think and behave and feel.

This book isn't any of that stuff. **How on earth would I have the right to tell you who you're meant to be or what you're meant to do? YOU ARE THE ONLY EXPERT ON BEING YOU.**

"Alright, Jennifer," I can hear you saying. "What if I don't feel like an 'expert'? What then?"

Here's the first truth from me to you: NOBODY feels like an expert. Ever. On almost anything. Know why? Because we each know our own most-secret doubts and mistakes and insecurities. And even though they can't, it sure feels like everyone can see the parts of us we're most afraid to show.

To become the woman you are meant to be—and you *are* meant to be amazing—you need someone (who thinks like you) to warn you of hidden pitfalls and point out the wonderful things you already are. You need a mentor—a trusted advisor who won't laugh at you, won't scold you, won't correct you. Someone who is ready to admit she doesn't know it all but sure wants to share what she *has* figured out...

Well, girls, a strong woman stands up for herself. A stronger woman stands up for us all. And that's what I plan on doing. I hereby offer you...ME—an I-get-it-because-I've-been-there (and sometimes it's been pretty and sometimes it SO has NOT) mentor, confidante, and friend. I'm not a role model—if, in your mind, that means "perfect" or "someone to look up to." You see, I'm not an object on a pedestal anymore than you are! And I certainly don't have it all figured out yet...but if you don't mind learning from someone who sees "mistakes" as lessons in socially awkward disguises, then we have some good times ahead.

Together, we're gonna tackle the big stuff, the things I *really* wish I'd known at your age—and the things that girls (from tweens to adults) most often ask me. I'm far from perfect. I can't promise that every answer will be flawless, but I can—and *do*—promise that every answer will be honest, empowering, and first-person spectrum savvy. Because you deserve that. We all do.

What's Ahead

- **Seeing Yourself**—What being "on the spectrum" looks like for us.

- **Need to Know (and Believe)**—Bulletpoint reminders to reread whenever you want to review the book's most important ideas.

- **Twenty Mighty Beautiful Mini-Chapters**—spectrum-smart info about your body, dating, friends, perfectionism, and more. It's part "typical world in translation," part *accurate* mirror where I get to show you the amazing person you already are.

- **Special Stuff**—smarts, done short and sweet (one's even from my dog).

- **Yellow Bricks**—Wisies from spectrum girls and women whom I count as friends, mentors, and mentees. Not only are you *not* alone—you are in some seriously amazing company. (Why "Bricks"? More on that in Chapter 1.)

- **Your Song**—Your celebratory send-off into this big ol' world of ours.

Your Invitation, Miss

This book is first-hand wisdom, real-life goof-ups (lots of those), light-bulb moments—it's the legacy of real relationship mistakes and triumphant discoveries, of trying on costumes and characters, of "faking it" too well, of self-punishment, of perfectionism, of fashion faux pas, professional snafus, and hollow apologies. It's mean girl drama and discovering the happy that's already within your reach. It's life goals and bras. It's lunchrooms and flirting. It's "normal"—explained in the way only we can understand.

In every word you read, trust that there is a knowing smile. In every subject we tackle, believe that truth and love are infused in every line. My words aren't reaching out to "them," they are reaching out to *you*—a hand to help you stand up straight and a voice to call you closer.

Yes, in a lot of ways, life is easier if you're "typical." To tell you anything less would be a lie. And everything I tell you—everything—is going to be true.

If you're a spectrum girl, you can probably mimic accents and gestures, and you may "fool" everyone by how well you "pass." But guess what? "Blending in" means not showing up. It means a lifetime of falling short of a goal that's not meant to be yours anyway: typicality.

You are NOT typical, thank goodness. And that's why, in a million subtle, abundant ways, YOU already *are* beautiful and strong. You are a gift to this world. A one-time only appearance. A perfect rendition of YOU in progress. It just takes a while to learn that...so I'm here to help give you a study guide. Because I get that. Now.

Think you've messed up too badly to go on? Nope. Happily, you cannot *actually* die of embarrassment (I know—I *am* the lab rat). More than that, mistakes aren't mistakes—they're lessons—if we learn from them. And let me tell you, I've learned a whole LOT of lessons along the way.

Who you are isn't one person—and she won't stay the same forever. If you're going to "just be yourself," you need to know that—just by showing up on this planet—you have permission to be an ever-changing, complicated, dynamic, MIGHTY BEAUTY. Once you *believe* that, once you *get* that, there is literally nothing that can stand in your way.

This book is NOT a textbook. It's not a collection of "general social conundrums" for guys *and* girls (that's *The Asperkid's (Secret) Book of Social Rules*), a style guide, or an "all about your body" book. (There are already plenty of good books like that.) It's not "report from clinical research" mumbo jumbo or superficial "Top 15 Ways to Steal the Spotlight!" That's not me. And I'll bet it's not you, either. No, in your hands is an invitation to join one of the world's most exclusive, most inspiring, most kind-hearted sisterhoods on earth—a sorority of heroines. Diverse women who will guide you in *becoming* your OWN authentic, precious self. With time, the world will FINALLY get to see the magical soul you are meant to be. And so will you.

Intense. Impulsive. Vivacious. Introverted. Perfectionistic. Inquisitive. Effervescent. Tentative. Impetuous. Measured. Complex. Genuine. Yearning. Fragile. Mighty. All at once.

That's you. That's us. That's the sisterhood on the spectrum.

Let me teach you some of our song, our melody. Then, add your harmony. And even if your voice is shaky or your microphone falls off, sing your hearts out, girls!

Because here, your voice is always precious. And here you most definitely belong.

Seeing You

You may recognize yourself (and some other awesome chicks) here:

I didn't see her Asperger's at first, as I did with your sons. You made the case, point by point, and asked me to stick around without judgment for a month or so. You were tired and had been through a wringer of psychologists and specialists, and I'll be honest, I thought you'd be wrong about her. You weren't. Every observation was spot on, and four years later, not only do I have no doubt about her Asperger's, you taught me what some of the world's best medical schools couldn't. (My kids' child psychiatrist)

This is the part where you find out who you are. (And how very beautiful she is.)

- Girls and women on the spectrum, like the boys and men, have special interests—topics to which we devote great affection, attachment, focus and time.

- Our interests are often similar to those of other girls and women. It's the level of intensity (often almost professorial), rather than the subject itself, that sets us apart.

- Facts don't usually change (except for "Pluto is a planet"), but people do. And that's scary. But the extreme focus we give to our interests is relaxing! Focusing our attention on reliable, predictable facts creates a sense of safety amidst the chaos.

- Most importantly, our special interests transport us to a distant time, place, species, or social scenario where interpersonal rules and customs can be "studied and mastered."

- Dictionaries for futuristic alien societies. Wiki boards all about hairstyles and social stratae from a specific time period. These are all "worlds" where we can imagine ourselves succeeding—worlds with fixed, clear, customs, clothing, and languages that leave whole lot less room for mistakes.

- Some of the more common "special interests" among women and girls include: history and historical fashions/recreations, animals (frequently horses or dogs), fantasy series (*Dr. Who*, *Harry Potter*, superheroes, *Game of Thrones*, *Star Trek*, etc.), rocks/minerals, magic/faeries/mermaids, and mythology. Often, we will hold onto loves from childhood that stay with us as we grow, like Disney, anime, and My Little Pony.

- Reading—voraciously—is another special interest (the act itself). Mixed within trendy fantasy novels, expect to see a love for classics—like *Anne of Green Gables* or Shakespeare or Jane Austen. Unlike male counterparts, it's the level of intensity, and a serious professorial level of knowledge, rather than the topic itself, that sets us apart.

- Girls often collect information on people and cultures rather than on things, which is why the "lists" we like to accumulate tend to include family trees/genaeology, timelines, language/translations, and maps.

- "Lining up" our figurine collections (Smurfs, American girl dolls, all of the books in a series) looks less "conspicuously spectrum-ish" than boys' rows of toy cars or trains, but the behavior is the same. And for the same reason. The enjoyment comes more from setting precise "tableaux"—a dollhouse scene or barn replica or Barbie wedding—rather than engaging in spontaneous, interactive play.

- Girls often hyperfocus on having one, all-encompassing "best" friend; later, this may evolve to an all-or-nothing self concept of being in a relationship—**words missing** or being able to "keep" a dating partner/spouse, at any cost.

- Many of us find it very tough to clearly distinguish an acquaintance from a close friend, or define what constitutes an actual friendship (we haven't had enough experience!).

- Asking a girl if she "has friends" (as many "experts" do) is silly. Most girls won't want to say "no." Admitting you don't have any friends feels shameful—it's telling the world there's something "wrong" with you (while you still want to convince the person asking to be nice to you!).

- Adults who want to help should ask girls to describe what they do with friends. Be on the lookout for diminished depth or lack of reciprocity: Is the relationship equal and a "two-way street?" Are conversations one-sided? How do we know these people are friends? Do we play together/hang out outside of school? Who does the asking? How often? Don't be surprised if we perceive a classmate, neighbor, or acquaintance who's never invited us out as a "best friend." That's an idea we'll vehemently defend, too, because facing the truth would just hurt too much.

- Girls will often take on the role of "boss" of younger children, needier/"new kids"/exchange students or of a precocious "little sister"—that's because peer-to-peer collaboration is MUCH harder.

- Look for "phases" of intense friendships with "breakups" or sudden ends. Being able to establish friendships is very different from being able to maintain them.

- We often come across (unintentionally!) as braggadocios know-it-all's, and frequently see compliments to others as insults to ourselves. Both behaviors reflect challenges with perspective-taking and low self-esteem, not arrogance.

- Parents or teachers may see girls playing "typically" with dolls or dress-up clothing. A closer look will usually reveal play scenarios that are restrictive to strict, special-interest-driven scripts (e.g. "Barbie" dolls who are actually reenacting Greek myths or news events).

- Spectrum girls are more likely to gather and memorize as much information as we can on social roles and sexual expectations. It's our way of compensating for what others pick up naturally—and it can be very dangerous.

- Looking or sounding "fashionable" is as common among girls on the spectrum as is disinterest in appearance. Girls on the spectrum are frequently fantastic mimics (often boosted by a love of theatre), can echo accents perfectly, and work tirelessly to assemble a "desirable" persona or "facade."

- Eating disorders like anorexia nervosa and bulimia should be considered "red flags"—they're indictors of perfectionist tendencies, internalized self-punishment, a need for artificial control, extreme rigidity and adherence to routine. More often than not, they are the rule among women on the spectrum, rather than the exception.

- Bathing/showering, hair brushing, shaving, wearing bras, and using feminine hygiene products can each pose a significant sensory challenge for spectrum girls. Discussing social stumbling blocks without addressing the underlying sensory issues sets us up for failure.

- Being overly "bubbly" and magnanimous is a common (yet exhausting) way many girls on the spectrum camouflage their social anxiety. Diagnosticians, friends, family, and teachers *must* look beyond the surface to determine organic from affect.

- If you've met one girl on the spectrum, you've met one girl on the spectrum. Yes, we have commonalities. And yes, we are as diverse and individual as any other group.

Quotealicious

IF SOMEONE CALLS YOU UGLY (OR DUMB, OR FREAK), YOU SHOULD SAY ... PURPLE TUNA FISH! BECAUSE IF THEY'RE GOING TO SAY SOMETHING RIDICULOUS, THEN YOU SHOULD, TOO.

Mermaids DON'T HAVE THIGH GAPS EITHER.

NORMAL. Typical. NOT SYNONYMS

- 1 -

Spelunking

Discovering the Typical Diamond You Already Are

Need to Know (and Believe)

- Being extraordinary is what creates value.
- "Normal" is a role played by many but lived by none.

Spelunking. Isn't that just the weirdest word? It makes me think of some nasty tree fungus or something. But it's not. Spelunking happens to be cave exploration. And guess what you can do while spelunking? Why, you can sluice, of course!

Nope, that's not a Dr. Seuss word, either. *Sluicing* (which sounds like *juicing*) is an old mining technique. You fill a wire box full of dirt and silt, then you slosh it around in running water to see if you've uncovered anything interesting. One minute you're digging through muck from an underground stream; the next minute you unearth these amazing, albeit really rough and dirty, little bits of treasure.

This, you may be thinking, is all very nice, but it has absolutely nothing to do with me. That's where you're wrong. It's not that I expect you to go grab a bucket and start hunting, but then again, let's say you did. I did, last spring. Through pail after pail of North Carolina's red earth, I picked and swirled and washed. And every batch was full of surprises. Before long, I had discovered dozens and dozens of stones: golden pyrite, silvery malachite, smoky quartz, rose quartz, sparkling mica. There were piles of them!

"We're rich!" my son yelled. Of course, I hated to disappoint him, but as lovely as they are, none of these stones are worth much money because they're very abundant—you know: normal, typical, common. They're everywhere. On the other hand, precious gemstones, like diamonds, rubies, and sapphires, are very rare. That's why they cost so much. If folks could dig them up in their own backyards, who would need a jeweler? Being extraordinary is what makes them valuable. And all we had was a bucket full of normal.

Here's where we get to you and me. Our brains operate in a way that is less common, a way that is called "autism spectrum" or "Asperger syndrome" (AS), and it's literally built into our hard-wiring. An AS label isn't good or bad. It's a description of our shared experiences. For example, you and I easily notice things others miss. We also miss things others easily notice. We feel emotions differently and sense the world differently. We think and fear and love and learn in ways that typical minds don't. The fact is, in many (though not all) ways, we are *not* common.

I understand wanting to fit in, to blend in, for it to be easy. Wanting to not worry so much about "belonging." Then again, I wonder if anyone really would be content being totally typical. Who chooses a hero "because he is *so* normal"? Who gets a compliment or wins an award or even lands a job by being run-of-the-mill? No one. That's because normal is an illusion; it's a role played by many but lived by none.

Look, you are in your own head twenty-four hours a day, seven days a week. You know every mistake you make, every doubt you have, every insecurity that wears you down. Dating, acne, the right way to stand or smile or dress for a party—normal people don't overanalyze all of this craziness, right? Wrong. Typical people don't feel normal a lot of the time, either.

Since I've been out of high school, I've made some discoveries. If by "normal" we mean "common," then it turns out, it's pretty normal to feel like you don't fit in at all. Everyone has strengths. Everyone has challenges. And everyone has behind-the-scenes fears that others never see.

Now don't get me wrong. Yes, some people do have an easier time naturally "playing well with others." That's an inborn talent. And envying others' abilities only wastes the time you should be honing yours. Are you a gamer? Personally, I stink at pretty much every video game I've ever tried. So if Minecraft is your thing, you definitely have some skills that I don't. That's OK. On the other hand, I can dance like nobody's business. Maybe you avoid dance floors like the plague and seriously believe you might die of either fright or embarrassment if you suddenly got stuck in a spotlight. That's OK, too. However, not being a particularly good gamer doesn't give me an excuse to avoid trying. Being terrified of dancing doesn't mean you get to hide on the sidelines. At some point, you have to get in there and say, "You know what? Who cares if I look ridiculous? I just wanna have fun."

Common is a relative experience. It's all about the surroundings. Whatever differences, talents, or challenges you experience from being on the spectrum are, well, pretty typical. I get you. So if you need to feel normal, hang out with me. We're both Macs in a PC world. Distinct. Innovative. Logical.

If you don't mind getting your hands dirty, think of this whole growing-up thing as spelunking and sluicing—only you don't have to hunt for anything "extra"ordinary. It turns out, you already *are* the discovery. You already *are* the treasure, as natural and as precious as a jewel. A diamond is, after all, just a lump of coal that handled a lot of pressure *really* well. So dust yourself off and get out into the light. You'll be amazed at how you shine.

2

Follow the Yellow Brick Road

Why You Don't Need a GPS to "Find Yourself"

Need to Know (and Believe)

- Lovability has nothing to do with anyone else…with whether they seek you or leave you.

- Good people reflect and magnify who you are, but lasting confidence (and contentedness) only grows from the inside-out.

- You can't expect anyone else to do *for* you what you aren't willing to do for *yourself.*

- We often mistake our most immeasurable gifts for shameful flaws.

- You are lovable. Right now. Without changing a single thing.

No Formula—Just a Road

Not long after I graduated from college, my grandmother sent me a book which proclaimed itself to be a "concrete set of do's and don'ts so you can actually land the guy of your dreams." I should've raised an eyebrow at that. Maybe two. The ridiculousness of that book still boggles my mind in about a thousand ways. You don't "land" a person. You land a plane. People can't be won like prizes, and even then, I knew it. Having the "right" people by your side doesn't suddenly make you more worthwhile. It just makes you more dependent, more vulnerable, and more terrified of being alone. I knew that, too.

Good people reflect and magnify who you are, but lasting confidence (and contentedness) only grows from the inside-out. That part…well, I said I knew it. Maybe you "know" it, too. Intellectually. But in our hearts, I don't think a lot of us believe it. I wanted, more than anything on earth, to feel powerfully, recklessly, unconditionally wanted. That, if I'd told the truth, was more important to me than any "perfect score" or list of achievements. Just imagine an oasis in a desert: you can see it out of reach…what you want most in the world—what seems almost possible—but it's just an illusion. That's happiness—that's "Who am I?" built on other people's approval…shaky, without substance. And for those of us who've spent a lifetime on the edges of "lovable," the want—the need—to be wanted and liked and included is too powerful to resist.

So guess what I did with that book my grandmother gave me? I read it from cover to cover. Why? Well, the answer may feel very familiar to other girls on the spectrum. Underneath my competent, confident exterior, I was also lonely, insecure, and sure that between my "hypersensitivity" and perpetual intensity, I was simply really difficult—if not impossible—to love. And that is a dangerous place to be.

Yes, your education matters (a lot). Your work matters. Your passions matter. Your friendships matter. Your sense of humor and your physical health matter. But wherever you fall on the human spectrum, the single most important thing to each of us—the emptiness that we will do anything to fill—is this:

We ALL need to know that—right now, without changing a thing—we are already lovable. That we are wanted—deeply, enthusiastically—precisely as we are. So listen up: You are loved. By me. Really. As you are. Right now.

For those of us on the spectrum, feeling lovable is a tall order. I get it. More often than not, our parents don't understand us. (My dad would walk away whenever I cried, and my mom didn't understand how I could be "so smart" and "so naive" at the same time.) Our classmates resent us and maybe even taunt us or insult us. Our coworkers leave us out or hang us out to dry. And the people who are supposed to cherish us may love so cruelly that we lose all perspective on what kindness is even meant to be. Why? Simple. The way we think, feel, understand, and love doesn't quite "fit." We know it. And so does everyone else.

"Just be yourself" we're told. But usually, it's survival of the generic out there. It doesn't feel very safe or smart—or even *possible*—to be authentic, to stop editing every thought and word…or to just give up. For sure, the world didn't like me whenever I was honest. I was the butt of terrible jokes—was even told to kill myself. I was also often misunderstood by the people closest to me.

So, c'mon! How are we supposed to feel comfortable when nothing (or at least not a whole lot) about fitting in comes naturally? Of course, there *are* things we can do to make life easier. We can learn the "(Secret) Social Rules"—I even wrote a book about the ones I figured out—but no one can (or should) be on-guard twenty-four hours of every day, evaluating her every gesture, second-guessing her every word. **That kind of life is an exhausting performance—a game of chess where you are trying constantly to anticipate other people's moves and plan accordingly. And you know what? I stink at chess.**

Here's what I *was* good at: school, dancing, annoying people, and sounding full of myself. Throughout life, experience had proven over and over again that given enough time, I could successfully irritate and tire out any coworker, friend, boyfriend, or family member into not just being done with me, but into seriously disliking me, and quite possibly even hating me. "Enthusiastically wanted" for just "being you?" No. That didn't make any sense at all.

Now, there is one important factor missing from this story—a major disadvantage I had that you don't. I didn't know I was an Aspie. For that matter, I had no idea what AS or autism was, let alone how it might relate to me. As far as I could tell (and everyone else said), Jenny was just an often-bossy, attention-loving, too-smart-for-her-own-good, over-dramatic crisis seeker. And without that spectrum identification, my life felt like a never-ending series of could-happen-at-any-moment catastrophes. There I'd be, doing my best at whatever it was I *thought* I was supposed to be doing—schoolwork, extracurriculars, studying (yes, studying) fashion magazines…heck, when my mom off-handedly mentioned that I didn't know how to flirt (I was fifteen), I tackled that "failure" with such gusto that, a year later, "flirt" was my nickname. Literally.

In other words, whatever it took to get people to like me, I tried to do—perfectly. So many of us do. The trouble is, "people" aren't a big blob of brainwashed clones with the same idea of what "likable" is. We're tilling at windmills. Chasing shadows. And even if by some miracle you *do* manage to pull off the "she's got it all together" persona—smart, accomplished, witty, charming (with effort), interesting, generous, physically attractive—you're doomed. If you're the best at everything, everyone else feels less by comparison.

The Trap

Spectrum girls, in particular, tend to be pretty hardcore perfectionists. We want to please other people. We want to be cared for. And dang it, we seriously need some approval—we, Aspies, have often had more than our fair share of unexpected "mess-ups," leading to more than our fair share of teasing, rejection, and insults. So it's not really surprising that, if we are told we do something well—maybe schoolwork, art, or even Lego building—that praise holds great power over our self-esteem. We attach our value to our performance, not to our personhood. **And there's the trap. Performances are judged by lots of people with lots of opinions (most of which are WRONG). Personhood just is. It can't be wrong. And YOU matter. Now. Already.**

But I'm going to be straight with you: for a very, VERY long time, I believed that was true—for everyone except me. There has to be a reason, we figure, for the serious dislike we seem to inspire over and over again...*something* that would explain how we could mean well but always end up making everything come out so wrong. After all, what has every disaster—*every* want-to-crawl-in-a-hole-and-die moment—had in common? It's not the other people involved. It's not the places where they happened. Nope. **The only common factor we can find in every disaster is ourselves.**

Costume Changes

So, I tried to "fix" things by hiding—sometimes actually (like in the woods outside my school), and sometimes hiding behind characters. That's a story I know is not mine alone. Like a lot of you, I got *really* good at pretending. At copying. At acting. At shape shifting. Mimicking phrases and body language. Being a coy flirt, an extroverted, social magpie.

And before long, it felt easy—well, at least, it sure felt good. My parents beamed in ways they never had before. I played the bubbly, beguiling, flirtatious role so well that I had a social calendar *full* of dates and was even picked as Social Chair for my college sorority (how ironic, right?). But none of it—none of it—was authentic. Which meant none of it was safe. A mask, after all, can be pulled off at any moment; and if that happened, there I'd be, exposed and unwanted. So I never, ever felt safe. I just felt fake. And afraid.

Guaranteed Success

Security. That was what I suppose I hoped to find in the book my grandmother sent: a foolproof, clear-cut road map to Acceptance Fantasyworld, like "plug and chug" math formulas. Do this, get that. Guaranteed success. No thinking required (and especially no overthinking, a specialty of mine.) Finally! A simple, Jenny-proof plan that made a whole lot of sense and wouldn't let me ruin everything…you know…just by being me. Except there was—and is—one hitch in that plan, one super-gigantic, entirely messed-up, couldn't-be-less-helpful, utterly wrong hitch: **Lovability has nothing to do with anyone else…with whether they seek you or leave you. It has nothing to do with what you do well or what you mess up. If you aren't happy within your own heart, you won't—I promise, WILL NOT—find lasting happiness in someone else…in anyone else. Ever.**

Why? The best explanation I ever heard came from a famously gorgeous dancer who said, "You can be the ripest, juiciest peach in the world, and there's still going to be somebody who hates peaches." No matter how appealing you are—in every and any way imaginable—nobody can be *everyone's* favorite. Nobody. No matter how perfect you try to be, if (down deep) you believe that you are whatever other people have called you (good or bad), you're standing on shifting sand…and you're going to fall. So how do you avoid the hurt? You don't. But believe it or not, that's not always a bad thing. Not fun…but not bad, either. It's a necessary part of the journey.

A Trip to Oz

I want you to imagine something now. Forget who you see in the mirror or what you worry about when you close your eyes. Instead, imagine you are Dorothy Gale, the girl in *The Wizard of Oz*. Remember her? Tornado sends her to magic land, she can't find her way, a witch and some freaky flying monkeys are hunting her? Yep, that Dorothy. OK, be her. And consider the situation.

After a long, confusing journey (in heels), after battling loneliness, disappointment, fear, loss, and insecurity, you've just discovered that no one is waiting behind the curtain. No one is coming to save you. No one ever was. Instead, the power to save yourself—to dream and do and be everything you've ever wanted—has been with you since your story began.

That, sweet friends, is the real tale I'm here to tell you. The real adventure you get to live. The real magic that is anything but make-believe. When Dorothy landed in Oz, she (quite by accident) killed the Wicked Witch of the East and was given a treasure—ruby slippers. They were lovely, of course, but let's be honest. Aside from being a rather fabulous fashion statement, those shoes didn't do Dorothy a lick of good. Who knows? Maybe they rubbed her the wrong way. Maybe they pinched. Maybe they made people stare.

Whatever they may have done, here's what we know for sure: Dorothy's gift couldn't have felt like much of a gift at all. From start to finish, all those slippers brought was a big bully, lots of havoc, and a huge amount of heartache. And then came the kicker: exhausted and hurting, Dorothy made the game-changing discovery that her nagging, gauche, uncomfortable gift secretly held the power she'd been seeking all along. What if she'd known that earlier? What if she had always known the value of what she possessed? Well, maybe Dorothy could have avoided the flying monkeys. She could have skipped the Scarecrow, Tin Man, Lion, and Wizard, not to mention the whole broomstick fiasco. Yes, everything would've happened a whole lot faster. But there'd be no story to tell. No adventure to remember. She would've missed out on the journey.

Each one of us is born with unrealized abilities to think and feel and do much more than we ever think we can. Like the shoes, we mistake immeasurable worth for hindrance and discomfort. We judge our endearing quirks as shameful flaws. We buy into the lies we are told and can't see the power that has been with us from the start.

Before you look to anyone else (including wizards) for love, brains, or courage, start a little closer to home. No matter how much you dress up or mess up or trip up, your truest self will remain hidden until you risk the journey to discover her. Along that road you can find trouble. And adventure. And love. And brilliance.

Truth? You are not going to find happiness by having the right prom date or report card or figure or friends. You are not going to find happiness until you are willing to start your journey as Dorothy did—alone. Because frankly, it's impossible for anyone else to know you or love you or respect you if *you* don't take the time to do it first...and then keep doing it. As I said earlier, you can't expect anyone else to do *for* you what you aren't willing to do for *yourself.*

How to start? Bricks. Yellow bricks. When Dorothy doesn't know which way to go, she asks for guidance from those who are already familiar with the route (a smart move). That, of course, is how she discovers the Yellow Brick Road in the first place—the path her journey must take. Unfortunately, real life is lacking clearly marked, technicolor bricks...which is particularly inconvenient because real life requires a lot more navigating than Oz ever did.

Alright, then. Let's build you your own road: a real, solid foundation. And like Dorothy's, your path is also made of individual pieces, each one strong on its own, fit together to help you find your way. Just follow the guidance of "those already familiar with the route!" You see, *your* yellow bricks aren't made of clay. They're the heartfelt words some of my favorite *spectrum* women want to be sure you hear.

You don't need a wizard. You don't need cool shoes (although I'm a sucker for shoes, I've gotta admit). You don't have to know how to do it all. Not now. Not ever. You just need to trust—even when it seems impossible or ridiculous or downright untrue—that everything you need to live a wonderful, meaningful, beautiful life is already within you. Let us, your spectrum sisters, help you find your way. We "get" you. And we will never, ever steer you wrong. Everyone has her own journey to travel, but you don't have to journey alone.

Everything you dream of doing or becoming…those things aren't somewhere over the rainbow—they are here now, and always have been. You are the magical, sparkling treasure. And the world is waiting at your feet.

Meeting other women on the spectrum is like looking into a mirror and for the first time in your life, actually recognising what you see.

~ Helen Wallace-Iles

3

No Spoilers, Sweetie

A Story About Stories...and a Relay Race

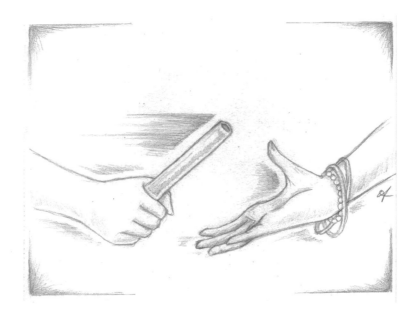

Need to Know (and Believe)

- In fiction, "spoilers" ruin everything. In real life, they *are* everything.

- Listening to someone does not mean that you accept their version of truth. It just means you have the confidence and courtesy to let them finish.

- Comparison is the greatest thief of joy.

- You can't be excited to grow up and also believe—on any level—that women have an "expiration date."

- Learn from those who start out before you. Teach those who come afterwards.

There are some words that sound like what they mean. Trudge. Slither. Moist. And "spoiler." Spoilers are rotten. They stink. And they ruin good things.

Just to be clear, I'm not talking about the spoiler on a car (in fact, I didn't even know that was a thing until last week). This "spoiler" is when someone reveals an important fact or event in a story without letting you discover it on your own. Example? Maybe you've just finished the balcony scene from *Romeo and Juliet* when your brother remarks, "Too bad they kill themselves in the end. Real downer." Thanks, dude. Might as well go tell someone that Darth Vader is Luke's father, too.

Of course, spoilers can slip out accidentally. Last year, I freaked out over a character's death on one of my favorite TV shows. Little did I know that (oops) my friend was recording the season to watch after she was done with chemo. She hadn't seen the episode yet, but she saw my Facebook post. Ugh. Social kablooey, for sure. Lesson learned, Jenny. No plot spoilers of any kind on social media. Check.

But you see, there's the difference. I felt sorry for "spoiling" some of my friend's enjoyment. On the other hand, when people stand on street corners shouting the end of the final *Harry Potter* book an hour after it's released, that's not accidental and it isn't funny. It's a power trip. It's a selfish "look what I can do just because I can" move that ruins far more than the ending of a story.

"Make-believe" has always been one of the most powerful ways human beings have to communicate their deepest fears, hopes, and beliefs. That's especially true for spectrum girls. Rich stories—the stuff of fantastic, time-traveling adventures in books, movies, and theatre—are alluring to lots of people, but are so in a particular, deeper way to us. Within nuanced other worlds like *Harry Potter*, *Mortal Instruments*, *Dr. Who*, *The Avengers*, musicals, dark fairy tales, or historical sagas, **we aren't losing ourselves—we're finding ourselves. We get to try on feelings that real life often denies us: alongside Hermione, Anne, Katniss, Annabeth, Luna, and other "heroes of our generation," there is a chance to be powerful, necessary, confident, unapologetically intelligent, brave…and deeply loved**.

Enjoying a story means enjoying the way the story unfolds. Slowly. Subtly. Characters in movies and books don't always do or say what *we* would. They don't always make the same choices we might (or even the same decisions the writer would!). It's the author's prerogative to create the narrative she wants. Plot twists. Heartbreakers. Unexpected solutions. All of it. Gradually, we learn how life really isn't all or nothing. That sometimes good people make bad decisions. That sometimes "bad guys" are just folks stuck without another choice. And along the way we discover little pieces of who we are, too. Of our opinions. Of our values. Of our wishes.

THAT is what spoilers really spoil. They don't just cheat us out of surprises. They cheat us out of becoming more of who we're meant to be. Usually. There is, however, one important exception to the "No Spoilers" rule. Just let me tell you a little story, and then you can see for yourself.

The Relay Race

Wriston Quadrangle is mostly rectangular; hence the name, I suppose (although I never actually thought about that until right now, to be honest). At its center is a lush, grassy lawn bordered by a somewhat unleveled sidewalk and edged by a series of grand, colonial-style brick buildings. Connected by arches, trimmed in white woodwork and black wrought iron, they're a delicious tableaux. A wonderful contrast of was and is, where the university's eighteenth-century birth somehow meshes seamlessly with the energy of new generations.

Wriston was the heart of my university experience, my home for four years. But for this story, what you really need to know is that every year in late October, Wriston is also the home of a totally unofficial, ultratraditional event known as "The SCUT races." In the cold night air, teams of "sophomores-currently-under-training" gather on the green, one group from each fraternity and sorority, surrounded by crowds of cheering (and much more warmly dressed) upperclassmen. Once the relay race starts, competing runners take one lap around the Quad, then pass a baton to their teammate for the next round.

During the weeks beforehand, you can look down from your window almost any night and see teams practicing. Two or three older "brothers" or "sisters" guide them, showing how to take shorter strides on the sharp turns, how to be careful of the steep downhill that can sometimes get slippery…and most importantly, how to hand off that baton without losing speed, or worse—dropping it.

That particular horror is still explained today, fifteen years later, in the Story of Jeff. The year he ran was the first ever that Jeff's fraternity, made up mostly of really big but not super-fast guys, was actually winning the race. Tall and quick, Jeff was the anchor. The final lap. People were screaming and chanting, breath steaming in the night air. This was actually going to happen! A simple pass to Jeff, and they would all watch him fly around the Quad to victory.

Only something went wrong. Somehow—whether he got distracted or nervous or who knows what—Jeff dropped the baton. And yes, his team lost. (And yes, when he tried to dip me on a dance floor a year later and accidentally dropped me on my head—giving me a concussion—his buddies wrote "Dropped her like a baton!" on his door.) But you can bet that no runner since hasn't listened to the Story of Jeff and cringed…and learned.

You see, **in real life, "spoilers" are exactly what we all need**. Think about it. How do the "coaches" know the gravelly spots the runners should avoid? Or how to pass the baton? They're not smarter. They're not just oddly gifted relay race runners. They're experienced. Not long before, those "coaches" were the competitors, nervously trying to pick up every tip before their own big night. Time moves forward. Seasons turn. And soon, this year's "SCUTs" become next year's mentors.

Someday, You Will Know

Life is a lot like those relay races. I've started before you, so I *will* notice pitfalls you can't have seen. But someday, you will know everything I know (well, the important things anyway). **Even when it feels like it, life is not an information-hoarding game where all the adults want to keep you in the dark for as long as possible. I promise.** As your "teammates who started first," our job is actually to get *all* the best answers—*and give them to you.* It's just that we gauge the pace. That's our job. We showed up on planet Earth first—it's nothing personal, it's nothing we chose. But we *have* been around for more of life, and we've seen beauty, and we've seen deep, dark ugly. A baby will lap at honey if you let her—after all, it's pretty and amber and sticky and sweet and oh-so-appealing. She doesn't know that it can kill her. The people looking out for her do. They will, of course, let her have the honey—when the timing's right—not simply when she wants it. That's love, not a power trip.

Really, I do understand the impatience and curiosity and frustrations. I couldn't wait to grow up (to be honest, I couldn't stand being a kid), and I know a lot of you feel that way, too. You don't want to be the little kid whom no one respects. I get that (although being older will not necessarily gain you respect—just responsibilities). But there's a flip side, sisters.

You can't be excited to grow up and also believe—on any level—that women have an "expiration date." That's a ridiculous notion which, first, puffs us up and sets one woman against another—causes us to roll our eyes at and disregard important role models. Then, before long, it stings and shushes us, just as we're getting comfortable in our own skin. Wrinkles come from thinking and feeling and smiling and crying and LIVING. Scars come from survival.

Growing older is a *gift* denied to many. Your sass, your smarts, your beauty, your appeal—they only get better with time and LOTS of experiences. There isn't some arbitrary window of time when you are worthwhile. You're not suddenly legitimate when you buy your first bra, nor do you "go bad" at thirty-five. Nope. It's just not true.

I happen to think Celtic myths paint a much savvier picture: they teach of the Triple Goddess, three entities in one deity. Woman is, they say, the Maiden, the Mother, and the Wise One—all at once. We are always more naive and less knowledgeable than someone. We are always meant to care for ourselves and one another. We are always a day ahead of someone else, always have something to teach. And that is why in fiction, **"spoilers" ruin everything. In real life, they are everything**.

Listen to those who've started out before you—that's all we are. Just girls like you who happened to show up earlier. No better. No worse. Learn from our successes and failures. Like the runners: one starts, the next follows. Each has her turn. Each learns from those who've run ahead, adds her own natural skills, then passes the baton to the next runner. There are slippery spots in life to avoid. Siblings, parents, teachers—they will try (not always successfully) to coach you. Sometimes the advice will be good, sometimes not. Either way, listen. And know that you, too, deserve to be heard, no matter how old (or young) you are or how different your opinions. Listening to someone does not mean that you accept their version of truth. It just means you have the confidence and courtesy to let them finish. The greatest minds can explore the nooks and crannies of someone else's very different ideas, disagree entirely, and remain respectful. In fact, only by being able to hear, understand, and speak about an issue to someone you disagree with (*without* insulting or disparaging her or him) will your opinion ever be seriously considered. It's the only way that our unique experiences, as girls on the spectrum, can open typical hearts and change typical minds.

You are a work-ever-in-progress. Be patient. Be-YOU-tiful as only YOU can be. Take the time you need to let your story unfold at the pace it will. Don't rush. You can't skip ahead anyway.

Remember how much of a story's power comes from slowly experiencing it? That's true for your story, too. Forgive yourself for not knowing what you didn't know before you learned it. You know what you know now. You are who you are now. So be her.

Don't bend to the world's suggestions that you be small or demure or conventional. Be vast. Contradict yourself. It's OK. Grow. Change your mind. Your life is happening for YOU. It's not a litany of achievements or disappointments to compare against those of anyone else. There's no measuring stick. Don't judge your Chapter 13 to my (or anyone else's) Chapter 36. Comparison is the greatest thief of joy. Know why? Because confidence isn't walking into a room thinking you're better or smarter or prettier than anyone else. It's walking into a room and being sure enough not to have to compare yourself to anyone else in the first place.

So, here's your SPOILER ALERT, girls: **You will come to know more. You will come to be more. And still… ALWAYS…whenever right now happens to be, you already are enough.**

That's one secret I'm very happy to tell.

- 4 -

Let Me Introduce You...
to Yourself

Need to Know (and Believe)

- Knowing yourself takes effort and courage. And LOTS of time.

- Your driving forces are those which need the most energy. Give them your time and attention, and life will feel better right away.

Ever notice how the smartest ideas—the biggest, deepest ideas—often come disguised as the simplest? Well, here's one for you, straight from ancient Greece: "Know thyself!" Two little words carved into the Temple at Delphi, where pilgrims would come from far and wide to seek wisdom. Not only sound advice, "Know thyself!" was believed to be so fundamentally necessary to any further "enlightenment" that it became the greeting called out to new worshippers. It's basic, but it's not simple. Ben Franklin wrote, "There are three things extremely hard: steel, a diamond, and to know one's self." Well, guess what? We can do hard things.

Of course, most of us think that we know ourselves pretty well. Then again, most of us would be wrong. Usually, the self we know is a phantom person—a girl made of shadows and other people's observations, not of raw potential and real ability. A litany of what you aren't or don't have, instead of a clear image of yourself—of all that you are and can do. The reflection in the mirror isn't you. (She's a jumble of judgments heaped upon a body.) The voice in your head isn't you. (She's a chorus of memories—of other people's opinions and other people's fears.) The character you wear to school, to work, or on a date or to a party? She's not you, either. (She's a blend of every mental note you've ever made.)

You are the beautiful person who sometimes feels afraid to say one more word or live one more day, because you might do it wrong. Again. You are also the sprite whose boundless will refuses to yield to that fear. You are unladylike laughter—brazen and bold. You are chili chocolate and tire swings, wild hair and quiet mornings. You are a tumble of spicy and sweet and sad and strange and lovely.

And you don't quite fit. Me neither. (Maybe that's because the box we're trying to cram all of our awesomeness into is just too darned small.)

In a world that often misunderstands so very much about us, just getting through the day is dizzying and distracting. Tiring. Being resilient is hard. Being a team player can feel downright unnatural. Life can be lonely. So we often look outward for appreciation—for everyone's else's approval (which means we also believe in their disapproval). Relationships—friends, dating—become desperate, imploding lifelines. What you do ends up defining who you are, instead of the other way around. We feel misunderstood—and we are...by ourselves.

It boils down to this: As you get older, the quality of your friendships will deepen. The friends you choose will "fit" better, too. Wonder why? Because once you dig in and get to know yourself, you'll have a much better idea of what kind of people you actually want in your life. But figuring that all out takes time—sometimes, a lot of time. In the meanwhile, go slowly and have some patience with yourself. Oh! And allow me to introduce you to the one person who ever *could*—ever *should*—fit the "best friend" bill. She's amazing. After all, she's you.

Detective You

If you're going to be able to discern—to really figure out—what you want, what you need (they're not the same), what you like, who you are, and (just as importantly) who you are *not*, you have to begin with a little detective work.

Start Your Engines

I'm not a scientist, so this isn't an official anything. It's just an observational tool, like a telescope pointing into the night sky. You, too, are made of endless constellations, clusters of ideas, feelings, motivations, and dreams. This part of you, your personality, is inborn. It has nothing to do with choice or even with being on the spectrum; after all, the spectrum isn't a lump of sameness. There are traits common among us, yes, but like everyone else, we are individuals, here with unique purposes, gifts, and needs.

Directions

"Try on" each of the following sentences. Put a checkmark next to those that feel "comfortable." THERE ARE NO GOOD/BAD ANSWERS.

Statement	Category	Check if it applies to you
I love words and language.	**A**	
I demand the best of myself at all times.	**B**	
I am full of energy.	**C**	
I am a helper.	**D**	
I am creative.	**A**	
I put a lot of energy into being prepared.	**B**	
I am comfortable being the center of attention.	**C**	
I am considerate without trying to be.	**D**	
I have a deep appreciation for beauty.	**A**	
I like routines.	**B**	
I feel at ease around strangers.	**C**	
I have a soft heart.	**D**	
I am quick to understand new ideas.	**A**	
I pay attention to details.	**B**	
I start conversations.	**C**	
I like being part of a team.	**D**	
I enjoy learning new ways of expressing myself.	**A**	
I take care of have-to-do's right away.	**B**	
I talk to a lot of different people at parties.	**C**	

I feel others' emotions deeply.	**D**	
I spend a lot of time thinking.	**A**	
I like order.	**B**	
I like spontaneity.	**C**	
It's really important to me that people get along.	**D**	
I am full of ideas.	**A**	
I prefer to follow a schedule.	**B**	
I am energized by performing.	**C**	
People feel comfortable around me.	**D**	
I prefer things that might be to things that already are.	**A**	
I am precise.	**B**	
I am enthusiastic.	**C**	
I find compromising easy. It feels natural.	**D**	
I am very curious.	**A**	
I am reliable.	**B**	
I seem to draw attention naturally.	**C**	
I get along with everyone.	**D**	
The arts are a big part of my life.	**A**	
I am a planner.	**B**	
I am talkative around strangers.	**C**	
I have no trouble sharing.	**D**	
I am adventurous socially.	**A**	
I like predictability.	**B**	
I am comfortable in front of crowds.	**C**	
I need everyone to get along.	**D**	

I come up with ideas others seem to miss.	**A**	
I follow my conscience, not my wants.	**B**	
I am outgoing.	**C**	
I am cooperative.	**D**	

Go back through the list. Tally up how many you picked from each category:

| A's: | C's: |
| B's: | D's: |

Meet the Engines That Drive You
(Remember, you are a MIX of them ALL.)

A's = Intellect and Openness

You are creative, imaginative, and philosophical. You're a thinker, a learner, a wonderer. You seek adventures, variety, and intensity in order to stay excited about whatever you're doing. Being around other people is energizing to you, for the most part. And a good deal of your alone time may actually be focused on communicating "you-ness" to the outside world: creating, writing, drawing, etc. Your curiosity about the world will always push you to explore and consider. You need ever-changing, broad-reaching outlets (often some creative art form) to express yourself—to record that you are here, you are alive, and you have something unique to say.

B's = Productivity and Order

You find great satisfaction in reliability and predictability. You're often most comfortable when things, events, and people are as you expect. Categorizing, labeling, and sorting make the world feel more manageable; these systems are super-important in helping you to feel on top of your work and your ideas. You tend to be more careful and reserved in your decision making. Results matter. You are hardworking and reliable, act dutifully, tend to be more self-disciplined (sometimes to extremes), and you like knowing that once you commit to something, you give it your all. It won't surprise you that a lot of spectrum folks will find "B" answers relatable.

C's = Enthusiasm and Extroversion

Extroversion does not necessarily mean that your self-worth is based on others' approval (that's a risk to be aware of, though). What it *does* mean is that you are energized by being around other people, and from things and experiences outside ("extra") of yourself. Think onstage performances. The life of the party— everyone knows when you've arrived or if you didn't show up. You are often talkative, a "joiner" who is active in your school and community because you genuinely like the excitement of group energy. You are an outgoing game-changer with ideas of your own and the enthusiasm to make implementing them fun.

One more thing: A lot of "experts" seem to think that people on the spectrum cannot be extroverts. Hogwash. I'd like to offer myself as evidence to the contrary, thank you. We can be whatever we are. Maybe it takes more energy for me (or you) to be social, maybe we get a buzz off of a really energetic, intense conversation with one person instead of always needing the crowd, and maybe we suffer a bit of a "social hangover" after being around a group. That doesn't mean we don't *like* it—it just means we need a little less of it than typical folks.

D's = Compassion and Politeness

Cooperative, helpful, gentle, and agreeable, that's you. On any given day, you're more interested in making sure everyone gets along than in having things follow your plans. You're typically quite calm and trusting—the easygoing one who is happy (not just on the surface but deep inside) as long as everyone's happy. You're more than willing to compromise in order to keep the peace, although you may do so at the expense of your own happiness. If tempers flare and you find that you can't "fix" or neutralize the problem, you're apt to shut down, walk away, or become loudly frustrated at what seems to you to be others' illogical behavior.

Pay attention to those sparks of creativity. They are little cries from your subconcious telling you to express yourself.

~ Rudy Simone

Power for Your Engine

Your most important gifts usually fall right in line with the things that make you happiest…and the things that make you happiest fall right in line with whichever "engine" drives your personality.

Think of each category as an emotional engine. To a certain degree, all four categories drive every person. But imagine, now, that you've got a set amount of fuel—that's **your energy, your time, your attention**—which has to be divvied up according to engine size. **Whichever engine has the highest score is like a pickup truck: it needs more fuel (in other words, more of your conscious attention) for your life to operate smoothly.**

That's true right down to the smallest number—which is more of a Vespa scooter.

You can't expect your soul to run on fumes. Want to feel safe? Want to feel happy? Want to feel satisfied? It's a simple to-do: **Once YOU KNOW WHAT YOU NEED, you can get what you need. Give your "big engines" (your strongest drives) the most fuel. And there's your power.**

When there are no words for all that's in you, and you feel something has to come out... ART happens.

– Sarah Vaughn

- 5 -

Playing Dominoes in Reverse

Know Where You Want to Go if
You Want to Get There

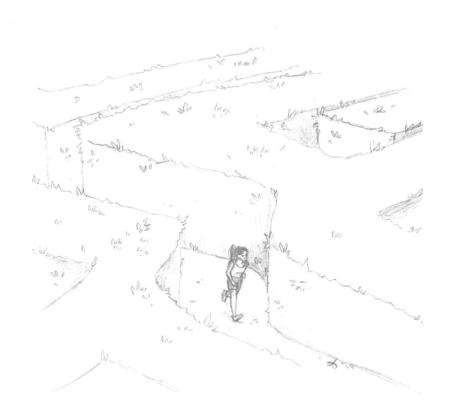

Need to Know (and Believe)

- We tend to think in a bottom-up style, starting with specific, concrete experiences, facts, and examples. Then, we spot trends, notice patterns, and discover the bigger concepts that link it all together.

- Every day, in many ways, you choose the life you live. We all do.

- You have to know where you're going in order to plan how to get there from here.

- Goals can (and should) change as you grow—as you go. But if you don't even know where the target is, you can't aim your energy, time, or money in the right direction. Really, you can't aim it in any direction at all.

- Plan for any goal the same way: Envision where you want to end up. Remember that life operates in a "DO–THINK–FEEL" cycle.

The first school subject to really give me a run for my money was geometry. Truth be told, I was fortunate in school; everything academic came easily to me. Mind you, I was also the consummate perfectionist, so "excellent" wasn't good enough for me—only "perfect" (even in the most challenging subjects) would do.

That would be why, at age thirteen, I completely freaked out. As a high school freshman, I had elected advanced geometry for my math course of the year, a bold placement that had to be staff approved. I wasn't being arrogant; I knew I could tackle this challenge, I wanted the transcript that went along with it, and I enjoyed pushing myself to learn new things (I still do).

However, this class threw me completely. Suddenly, we were memorizing random theorems about abstract rules which seemed unimportant and disconnected. For example, we read that a trapezoid is isosceles if, and only if, the base angles are congruent. OK, well, I understood the words, and the little picture in the textbook looked right, so, if they said so…but trust me, there was no real learning happening.

Then, to make matters worse, we were expected to apply these random theorems in real time when solving problems that didn't look anything like the original instructional illustrations. I was lost and, worst of all, I truly didn't understand what I didn't understand. **How do you ask for help when you don't even know what's confusing you?**

Looking back, I can see that it wasn't the material that didn't make sense to my brain. It was the way the information was being presented. As far as I was concerned, everything was happening backwards. Well, actually, it should've been backwards but was forwards instead. Oh, forget it—even this explanation is confusing! I'll just show you what I mean.

Geometry involves a lot of "proofs." You will either remember (from your own experience) or discover that these mathematical problems begin with a diagram of some lines or shapes, as well as some "given" facts that are true about the picture. Last, you are told what conclusion you have to prove, step by step, using the information provided and a combination of mathematical "laws."

One at a time, you list what you know or have proven as "Statements," simultaneously noting *how* you've arrived at each point under "Reasons." Here's the start of an example:

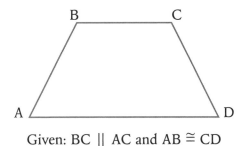

Given: BC ∥ AC and AB ≅ CD

Prove:

$$\angle A \cong \angle B$$

Back then, as far as I could tell, the only thing this kind of problem had going for it was that at least I knew where I was supposed to end up. On the other hand, how the heck I was supposed to move forward from step 1 almost always eluded me. At the time, I had no idea why this was so hard. And certainly, my instructor couldn't understand why I wasn't acing her class as I had previous math courses. So the teaching approach didn't change…and neither did my frustration level.

Bottoms Up

Let me stop for a moment. This chapter isn't *really* about geometry. But, by now, you've probably gotten the hang of the way I explain new ideas. Generally, I tell you about an experience (or two or three) from real life, and then connect them with one, bigger idea. It's like a building a table. You can lay out the large top, then stick in the supports underneath (that's **top-down**), or you can do it the other way around. Start one by one with the legs, then cap them together with a single top piece. Building up from small parts to one, unifying whole. Joining them. That's a **bottom-up approach** to thinking that usually feels more natural to those of us on the spectrum.

Neurotypical minds (and geometric proofs!) work the other way around: top-down, based on deductive reasoning, which is usually thought of as a skill that develops without any teaching or training. And for nonspectrum thinkers, that's mostly true. They see a fact—maybe a facial expression, maybe a social situation, maybe a geometric law—and easily link it to a clear, logical conclusion.

Only, "clear" is a relative term. Our spectrum minds operate differently; we don't make the same mental leaps others do. So "obvious" to them isn't "obvious" to us.

Generally, we understand things, people, ideas—life—using inductive reasoning. We go from the bottom-up, starting with specific, concrete experiences, facts, and examples. Then, we spot trends, notice patterns, and discover bigger concepts that link it all together.

All in all, having different methods of thinking is a good thing. If we lived in a world where everyone arrived at the same conclusions, we would be without creativity, problem solving, or curiosity.

There is, however, one complication: the world is trying to support us and teach us…*backwards*. Neurotypical teachers, friends, mentors, and parents are all showing us how to set and achieve goals in the most opposite way (top-down) to which our brains actually work (bottom-up).

What This Has to Do with Dominoes (and You)

As you grow up, you find that most (certainly not all, but most) of the people and things in your life are people and things you've said "yes" to…you've allowed in…and then keep choosing. **Every day, in many ways, you choose the life you live. We all do**. And every choice we make—little ones and big ones, both to our benefit and to our detriment—are the expressions of your wants: to be accepted, to be valued, to be congratulated, to feel special, useful, creative…that's not good or bad. It just IS.

All of this boils down to one, big "GIVEN": **YOU have more power than you realize**. You won't always get what you want. No one does, and even if you're disappointed, your life will not be miserable due to a lack of a new car. **Needs**, however, are a very different story. **When we talk about needs, we're talking about the things you require to live a healthy, happy life.** You've already identified your driving personality forces. **Now that you know what kind of decision maker you can be, and that you have a right to say "no" to anything you don't want or need, let's figure out how you're going to live a life you're proud of—from the bottom-up.**

Dominoes: Causing the Chain Reactions You Prefer

When you turn on a GPS system, you enter the destination, right? **You have to know where you're going in order to plan how**

to get there from here. Well, instead of solving that geometry proof from start to finish, it would've been *much* easier for me—and probably you—to start at the end and work backwards. If I want to prove this, I have to show this. If I want to show this is true, I have to show why. Start it in reverse, and you won't waste time lost and confused.

Think of it this way: if I ask you to buy the groceries for dinner but don't tell you that I want to make chicken pot pie, you may very well bring home the ingredients for lasagna. You've probably heard it said, "Fail to plan and you plan to fail." That seems to be a pretty common blunder for a lot of us on the spectrum. Maybe you don't actually map out the step-by-step process you'll need to follow to get your homework done on time—and lo and behold, week after week, it doesn't get turned in, or it sure isn't an example of what you really can do, OR you end up melting down because you're so stressed and mad at yourself—again. Or it might be something much bigger. For me, my senior year of college came along and I really had no idea what I ought to do next. What feels like a world of choices to a neurotypical is often a big pile of overwhelming confusion to us. So, despite a fantastic grade point average, I watched all of my friends head off to law school, medical school, and to pursue doctorates...and I had nothing.

Goals can (and should) change as you grow—as you go. But if you don't even know where the target is, you can't aim your energy, time, or money in the right direction. Really, you can't aim at all.

Often, the life stories of (very bright) spectrum adults include wasted years of "wandering time"—beginning and abandoning academic programs with degrees unfinished, unable to find or keep any sort of truly satisfying or lucrative job.

The trouble isn't that we're "dumb" or incapable. Usually, the issue is that we haven't taken the time to really nail down our wants, needs, and goals—so we're certainly not living lives full of smart, strategic, empowered choices. We're sort of...drifting. Like seaweed on the ocean. Just being carried this way or that. Aimless. And the result is **always** periods of depression, of dependence on family, of personal disappointment, and *very* often also includes drugs, drinking, eating disorders, self-mutilation, and controlling or abusive relationships.

It's really this simple: You deserve to **be the director of your story, not just an actor in the show.** Want to decide which college to attend? Whether to date the new kid? Get your homework or taxes or even your mother's birthday gift ready on time—for once? You've got to set the goal. Plug it into the GPS. Then start moving.

Imagine setting up a domino run: You start with the very last domino that will (eventually) fall, then place the one which will knock it down, then the domino to knock *it* down…and so on, all the way back to the starting point. When it's actually "go" time, the whole line will fall in the "correct" order, from start to finish.

Plan for your goals (whether it's to do well on a test or to catch someone's eye) the same way:

1. Envision where you want to end up.

2. Remember that life operates in a "DO–THINK–FEEL" cycle.

    a. You DO something.

    b. What you do (and don't do) causes you and/or others to THINK about you and about those actions.

    c. Those thoughts cause FEELINGS—either positive, negative, or neutral—about you and/or what you've done.

    d. The feelings cause you (or other people) to take new actions. You're right back at "DO."

3. Set up your "chain reaction" with your goal as the final "DO" or "action."

4. Work backwards from there.

5. If something in your life isn't going as you'd like, jump in at any point and change what's happening by DOING something new.

The whole process looks like this:

Cause the Chain Reaction
YOU want: By planning it in
Reverse.

'DO
²THINK
³FEEL
⁴DO

1. Determine what you want to
happen (that's the "do").

PLAN

d t f d

3. Then, ask yourself what thoughts
would have to precede those feelings.

PLAN

d t f d

4. What can you DO to create
these thoughts?

PLAN

d t f d

2. Next, decide what feelings (f) - yours
or someone else's, could make that
do/action possible.

PLAN

d t f d

5. Now...
MAKE IT HAPPEN!

DO IT
IN REVERSE

d t f d

Now, let's give it a go. Say your goal is to save enough money to buy a new book.

- For book buying to happen, you must first **feel** capable of saving some money.

- For you to feel capable of saving, you must first **think/believe** you can earn your own money.

- For you to **think/believe** you can earn your own money, you must first **do this**: fill out a job application and start your part-time job.

- That's the whole shebang!

  ° Goal: Buy a new book.

  ° Plan: Fill out job application and start work. Save money from pay. Buy book!

  ° GOAL ACHIEVED.

You only get one life, but you do get lots of chances to make plans…and make a mess…and then make some more plans. Recall your engines—your driving forces that need to be first priority. Keep them in mind, and be bold and brave in whatever goals you set. Always follow your heart. And never, ever forget to use that fabulous bottom-up brain.

– 6 –

Decisions, Decisions

What You Choose Is What Continues

Need to Know (and Believe)

- You are powerful.

- We are in charge of the choices we make and the consequences of those choices.

- Sad is a mood. It's real, it's hard, but it's temporary. And you *can* do hard things.

- You are the heroine in your own life story. Act. Don't be acted upon.

- Sometimes, painful experiences are the only way to learn the lessons we didn't even realize we needed to know.

More Detective Me: Check Yes or No

Think back to your "engines," your driving forces. They have to be fueled for you to be happy. So you have to choose the right "fuel"—experiences, people, and habits that feed your heart. On the other hand, you *also* have to choose who and what *not* to include. Believe in people's actions, not their words. If someone makes you feel uncomfortable or unsupported or burdened, that's a drain on your engines. Make a choice. Move on or tell them to move on. Because girls, **you are not helpless**. **You are POWERFUL**.

Examine what you choose and what you don't, because what you accept for yourself *will* continue. Sleep. Good food. Vulnerability. Healthy boundaries. Blame. Responsibility. Generosity. Risk. Adventure. Courage.

What are you agreeing to *today*? Why? What do you really desire? Is there another way to fulfill that desire? Girls, in your life, I hope that you will allow yourself to be sad, but never allow yourself to be unhappy. I'd rather you be neither, of course. I'd love for every day of your life to be filled with adventure and joy and anticipation. But that's not going to happen. And my telling you so isn't a buzzkill/gee-thanks-a-lot-Jennifer. It's a friend being honest because you deserve it and can handle it.

Sad is a mood. It's real—but temporary. Unhappy, though...well, that's a state of being. And it's an awful, stifling place to be.

Real life isn't a little angel on one shoulder and a little devil on the other, both whispering in your ear and vying for your attention. That's just not how it works. Instead, as you get older, you'll find that you must make choices where the *good* decision feels absolutely terrible...and you'd give *anything* to avoid certain hurt for an uncertain "possibly improved" future.

Let me give you an example. There's an old country song called "Unanswered Prayers" that tells the story of a man, now grown. One evening, he accidentally meets a woman who, years before, had been his first love. They are both married to other people now, but upon seeing her, the man remembers how desperately he had once hoped, with every atom of his being, that this woman would be his forever and ever.

I remember being told that life isn't like a drive-through restaurant where we can order up whatever we want. You can't just walk up to a guy at a counter somewhere and say:

"Hi, I'd like this particular boyfriend for the next, umm, 40 years, please."

"OK, and would you like marriage, career, and kids with that order, miss?"

"Sure. Why not?"

For the man in the song, the twist is that his prayer hadn't gone unanswered. It just happened that the answer was someone else— someone, it turned out, he'd love even more. But let's be honest. When your heart is actually breaking, that's your reality— not some future possibility that you can't even fathom. So, I'd reimagine the drive-through a little bit closer to this:

"Hi, I'd like this particular boyfriend for the next, umm, 40 years, please."

"No. Sorry. Not going to happen that way."

"Excuse me? I *said* 'please'."

"Yup. Still not happening that way. Don't worry. There's great stuff ahead, but not with this person."

"I don't understand! I don't want to lose what makes me happy! I don't want to feel lonely, or rejected, or sad. I really, really don't want to hurt! I'm happy! I want *this!*"

"I know, miss. Sad stinks. But unhappy is worse."

"What! What's the difference?"

"Sad is a mood, miss. It hurts like heck, but it will pass. Unhappy is much bigger. It's regret and longing and feeling trapped and scared and alone. And it doesn't go away. And you know you deserve better."

At many points ahead, you *will* be faced with situations that make you want to stomp your feet and bang your fists and yell, "But I don't wanna!" It may be "I don't wanna break up" or, "I don't wanna move" or, "I don't wanna change schools" or, "I don't wanna follow the rules." But it won't matter. I get that. I've been there so many times. I've been there as a kid, teen, young adult, and parent. Choosing to stay behind while my entire school music department went on a cross-country adventure because I had a hugely important advanced-placement end-of-year exam the day after the return, and I knew I'd be too exhausted to give it my all. That'd mean a less impressive college application and a year's worth of serious academic dedication thrown away. Yet not going on the trip would mean I'd be left out of the memory making, and, I feared, left out of everything in times to come.

In the end, I didn't go on the music exchange; instead, I cried the whole weekend. Come Monday, though, I rocked that exam. And while there were a few stories I'd not be able to be a part of, nothing else changed because I'd been absent from one adventure.

There have been so many other examples. Romance that began like a fairytale and turned out to be anything but…meaning, I had to end a relationship with someone I still (desperately) loved.

And even though it would cause deep sadness and shatter dreams I'd held precious, that breakup was the right decision.

Maybe you wonder why I allowed so much to go so wrong before I put a stop to it? I'd have told you love, I'd have said hope. But the truer answer would be fear—fear of unbearable loneliness and searing pain.

By design, pain is a teacher. After all, we are free to make our own choices in this world. That doesn't mean we're free from the consequences of our choices. After an "ouchie" or two as babies, we learn what hurts, and the fear of it protects us. Avoiding a burn from a hot stove is a good thing. Avoiding a cut from a sharp knife? Also good. But when the pain we fear is emotional—sorrow, loneliness, shame—there's a difference. **That fear doesn't protect us; it paralyzes us like a caterpillar too afraid of change to climb into the chrysalis. It doesn't know that wonder is ahead, just that the familiar will be gone.** We're much the same. Terrified of heartache, we bury our heads and avoid tough decisions. We take what other people dish out. We surrender our dignity, endanger our safety, and cut ourselves off from life's most magical opportunities. We ignore the fact that, sometimes, painful experiences are the only way to learn the lessons we didn't even realize we needed to know.

There's an additional factor for those of us on the spectrum. Almost without exception, we find decision making to be really, really overwhelming. Paralyzing, even. So, frequently, we make the decision to *avoid* making a decision. We procrastinate. You know, "play ostrich." We ignore the issue no matter how big or bad or loud it is until one (or both) of our choices are no longer available. And then, we say, life made the choice for us. But it isn't true. That's the way to actively choose to be a passive character in your own life story. To live a life dictated to you. Sure, "letting life happen to you" might seem easier. Don't pick and choose, don't hurt anyone's feelings, don't commit to one thing or another.

Guess what? Doing nothing is a choice, yes, but girls, it really isn't an option. Avoiding something or someone—conflict, homework, a breakup—because it's uncomfortable or unpleasant won't work either. You'll end up in trouble, for one. And if you don't, you'll end up being controlled, not loved—or even liked. No one likes a pushover. Not even the pushover herself.

I know what it's like to think, "But I can't. I *really* can't do this. It's too (insert adjective—maybe sad, maybe embarrassing, maybe hard)." I get what it is to cry so hard and so long that your eyelashes stick together like wet, woven spiderwebs. I know what a broken heart feels like. To lose a parent. To watch your best friend die. To be physically and emotionally humiliated or hurt. To wish you could just stop being. To be so lonely that you ask Santa for a friend for Christmas. To be so afraid that you'll accept anything—believe anything about yourself—just to keep from being alone again. Whatever you think you have. It's OK to cry—hard. It's OK to melt down. Just don't unpack and stay there forever. Breathe. Then remember, whatever it is that's going on—whatever decision or circumstance you're facing—you *can* make it to the other side. Think back. In one way or another, you've gotten through every single bad day you've ever had. Every single one. Maybe it wasn't always pretty, but you always made it. And I'd have to say that 100% is a pretty good track record.

OK, listen up:

No one is coming to save you. No one is coming to take care of you or do it for you or fix everything every time. You were not born a winner. You were not born a loser. You were born a chooser. Act instead of being acted upon. This life is 100% YOUR responsibility. You get to be the heroine in your own story. So, no matter what happened beforehand, make a decision. You always, always, always have a choice. Stand up and speak up, even if your voice shakes. Because, mighty girl, you've got this.

"No" Is a Complete Sentence

People Pleasing vs. Pleasing Yourself

Need to Know (and Believe)

- "No" is a complete sentence. It doesn't require apology or explanation.

- There are usually ways that you can stick to your beliefs without offending others.

- Recognize. Reply. Recommend. Or use a code word.

- Sometimes, the scariest, saddest decisions are the very best you'll ever make.

Since we're talking about making choices, here's something that *a lot* of girls aren't ever taught: "no" is a complete sentence. It doesn't require explanation. It doesn't require excuses. All by its lonesome, "no" can be enough. Want proof? Just listen to a two-year-old speak. More than any other word, you'll hear her shout, "No!" That's because, for the first time in her little life, this person has discovered the ability to exercise power over the world around her. "No!" she doesn't want green beans. "No!" she doesn't want help getting dressed. "No!" She knows what she wants and this—whatever *this* happens to be—is *not* it. Of course, the adults she loves and adores will try to coax her. They may turn a cold shoulder, expecting her to follow where they go. They'll ask her to "Do it for me. Pretty pleeease?" They'll tell her she's being foolish. Babyish. They may even offer "bribes."

And you know what happens? She learns—we learn—that we can be talked out of our "no." That we have a price. That good girls go along with what's asked of them. We learn to please others rather than ourselves. To believe that we *are* silly. That being opinionated is being difficult. We learn to give in to teasing. To agree to something we don't like or are afraid of in return for approval—or love. That, dear ones, is a very dangerous pattern. The same words spoken to little girls—"Come on, please? I love you. Don't you trust me?"—are spoken to bigger girls, too. Only as we grow up, the stakes become much higher than green beans.

The truth is, when you find yourself stuck between making a "good" choice and doing something that you hope will get you "liked" (or "loved"), or at least "included," good sense goes out the window fast. That doesn't make you weak or desperate. It makes you human. Trust me, this isn't some preachy, after-school movie about peer pressure. It's just the truth. When you're used to being lonely, teased, or left out, it's a lot harder to make choices that will make you proud. Going along with…well, almost anything…? Suddenly, it—whatever "it" is—doesn't sound foolish. It sounds tempting. I know. I've been there, too. Lots of times. And I hate to say this (because I *really* don't want to be the finger-wagging adult), but I love you too much to be anything but straight with you: Every time I agreed to something I didn't really want to do—every time I went along with something that made me feel afraid or cheapened—every single time, I gave away a little piece of my dignity. And once you start down that slippery slope, girls, it's only a matter of time before you'll take any name, insult, or punishment hurled at you (doubly true if it comes from a "friend" or someone you love). After all, you'll think, who am I to deserve better?

The answer, of course, is that you are made of stardust and possibility and love and goodness. And you deserve only grace, kindness, and respect. But for now, a little something more immediately useful may help.

The Solution: How to Be True to Yourself (and Keep the Relationships You Want)

See if this setup sounds familiar: someone offers you a cigarette and says, "What's the big deal? Everyone smokes." You're supposed to reply by saying (bet you can practically chime right in now), "Yeah? Well, I'm not everyone. I can think for myself." Or someone says, "I love you; I want to show you how much I love you," and you're supposed to answer, "But if you loved me, you'd wait." Oh boy (shaking my head and rolling my eyes). *This* would be just one of the major places adults fail you: we give you lame tools (this one's called "reverse peer pressure") to handle situations we've actually been through. Girls, every adult woman you know has faced those moments—and none of us got through them (successfully anyway) by using pithy health-class one-liners.

In *real-life* moments, what you want to happen is actually two very different things. First, you want to be able to say "no" to something in particular and feel that your word is respected. Second, you don't want to come off as stuck-up or insulting. Reverse peer pressure strategies will get the "no" across but usually sabotage the other end of things. (They sound arrogant—the I-think-I'm-so-much-better-than-you sort of thing.) The thing is, you don't have to be snobby to be confident. You don't have to be uppity to stick to your guns.

Here, my friends, are two strategies that will allow you to keep your decisions—and whichever relationships you choose—in tact:

- triple "R" (Recognize, Reply, Recommend)

- code word.

Triple "R" (Recognize, Reply, Recommend)
Recognize
First, you need to be able to spot, with confidence, when you're being or feeling pressured. Think of it as catching faulty logic—by knowing *how* people most frequently rearrange a situation to suit them, you become a sort of human lie detector. (Even better, this is actually something you can use in, say, debate club or practice on advertisements.) So let's arm you with information. Call it "peer pressure" or call it "logic FAIL"—just be sure you **recognize** it—and call it something other than TRUE.
Three common ways others will try to influence you:

- **The Bandwagon Technique**: In the days before cars, political candidates would hire large horse-drawn wagons in which to ride though city streets. It was a publicity stunt. Political signs, music playing, and an invitation for all supporters to "jump on the bandwagon" and join in the fun (which, by that point, had usually become a full-blown party). **"If lots of people are doing it, the idea must be a good one."**

  Logic FAIL: Popularity has nothing at all to do with whether an idea is true or good. Want proof? Look to Nazi Germany during the Second World War. Or to the American slave trade. Or commercials advertising "healthy" cigarettes in the 1960s. (And more often than not, "everybody" isn't "doing it" anyway. I *promise*.)

- **Appeal to Fear**: This is when someone makes your fear the consequences of not doing what she wants. It's your classic "if you don't X, then Y (which is awful or upsetting or scary) will happen." For example, "If you don't…kiss me, steal the answers, wear these jeans, etc., then no one will like you— I'll tell everyone you did a lot more than that—everyone will think you're a loser, etc." And let's be honest. Creating fear is an effective method for forcing action. When you are afraid of something or of someone, you're much more likely to make a decision you wouldn't otherwise make. **"Do what I want you to do, or terrible things will happen."**

  Logic FAIL: Fear tactics have nothing to do with truth. They're all about control. Don't use this particular body wash? It does NOT mean you're going to have body odor. Don't drink when everyone else does? You won't be thought of as a loser. You'll be the very popular designated driver (who also has other people's respect).

- **Exigency**: Hurry! Limited time offer! Deadline is tonight! Only the first twenty customers can win! Ugh. Enough. That's way too many exclamation points. What's with all the panic? Exigency, that's what. It means using nothing more than a sense of "do it now—it's your only chance ever— you'll always regret this decision" urgency to get someone to do something. Look for these clues that exigency is at work against you: an action is requested/suggested/demanded AND you hear "time" or "speed" words—now, hurry, fast, last chance. **"Do what I'm saying quickly (before you actually have time to think about it carefully) or you'll regret it."**

  Logic FAIL: Exigency is all about a false sense of need. You're being forced to make a decision—to respond—to someone else's made-up timetable. It's the most classic emotional blackmail used by companies who want your money, by politicians who want your votes, and by peers…who want something else. Exigency rattles you and undermines clear thinking. **Important doesn't always equal urgent.**

Reply

Give your "no" firmly and clearly, leaving no room for "maybe" or persuasion. A wishy-washy "no" can be taken for "push me just a little more and you'll get a yes." (That being said, if you aren't certain of your decision, you don't *have* to be ready with one. Just say that you need more time or more information, that you'll think about it, and that *you* will tell *them* when you've made up your mind—until then, no more discussion.)

How? Saying "No" doesn't mean you are being rude, it doesn't mean you are being difficult or disagreeable, and it doesn't mean everyone will hate you, either. You don't need to scream it. You don't need to slam your fists like you did as a toddler. You can (and should) be polite and even kind, if possible. (And even if it's "not possible," you *still* get to say "no"—*however you need to say it.*) Here are a few examples of how to do it:

- Maybe you've been asked on a date by someone in whom you're not really interested. (Every sincere question deserves a sincere answer.) Try "I really appreciate your asking me, but no thank you."

- Maybe someone wants to copy your homework. You can say, "I understand you need help, but I'm just not going to say 'yes' to that."

- Maybe someone passes you a little something to smoke, and you know better (*please* know better!). "Thanks, but no thanks" will do just fine.

Recommend

Suggest something else to do either now or in the future. "You know, I'm not really into that. How about we (insert alternative here) instead?" This shows that you're not snubbing the person, you're just nixing the activity.

Code Word

Sometimes you need a lifeline. A wingman. Somebody to help you stick to your principles, even if you find yourself caught in a really tough spot. That's when a code word can help.

Years ago, I told my niece and nephew that if they ever found themselves at a party where kids had been drinking, they could *always* call me—no matter the time—for a ride home. All they had to do was phone my cell and say our code word. Once they used it, I wouldn't "tell" and I wouldn't judge. I wouldn't even drive right up to the party, if they preferred. I'd happily pick them up a few doors down, if it made leaving less obvious.

Here's how it works: Choose a code word that's distinct but common enough that you could add it into any phone conversation without your meaning being clear to everyone around you. For example, let's say you're at a friend's house and something— anything—about the situation has gotten too uncomfortable for you. All you do is call/text your "safe" person (could be a parent, an older sibling, an aunt/uncle) with what seems to be an insignificant message. Maybe it's this: "For dessert, can we have pistachio ice cream?" *Pistachio* is the code word (not your usual choice, so the receiver is sure it's no accident), and upon hearing it, the safe person acts as you've both already planned: he or she says loudly or writes in ALL CAPS to forget the ice cream, you were supposed to be home an hour ago! You'd better get a ride, walk, or expect to be picked up immediately. And sure, if you want, you can even act like you're really annoyed at having to leave, even though that's your actual goal.

The advantage to this plan is that anyone around you will think you're in trouble. That you've got to leave NOW. The truth is that you're keeping safe. You're abiding by your conscience. And no one feels insulted. Good stuff, all around. There is, however, one promise you have to make in exchange for the safety the code word offers: After you're home, you have to think about the details of the situation. You need to evaluate who and what caused the discomfort, and decide whether that's a one-time bummer or a symptom of a relationship you really don't need in your life.

Falling into Place

And guess what else? If, at any point in any situation, something inside you begins to feel uncomfortable, scared, or just "not right," ANY "YES" is allowed to turn into a "NO." That doesn't make you a "tease" or a liar. It doesn't mean you've broken a promise, either, because above all, the only lasting promise you need to make is to your own conscience.

However you say "no," the only rule is this: you need to be able to say "no" without apologizing for your feelings—without caving—even if "no" means disappointing someone you care about or makes you feel embarrassed or uncomfortable. Even if you are tempted to say "yes," once you decide "no," there can be no pleading or forcing or punishing. That's not flattering attention. It's flat-out rude.

And one more thing: Let's say you're driving along a highway, meant to get off at Exit 23. Well, you happen to get lost in thought, and when you look up, you realize you're passing Exit 24. You've missed your turn. What do you do? Do you keep driving and thinking, "What's the use? I've already gone wrong… everything's ruined anyway." Or do you look for the first chance to turn around, head back in the right direction, and go where you're supposed to go? Obviously, the second is the better choice. Well, the same is true in life. If you forget something or get mixed up or you completely mess up, all is not lost! Don't quit and keep driving off into the sunset, for Pete's sake. Turn around. Change course. Refocus your aim and keep moving. Even if it takes a bit longer to get there, your destination still awaits you.

Part of growing up involves learning that being brave means being afraid but doing it anyway. It means learning that sometimes, the scariest, saddest decisions of all are the very best you'll ever make. It means trusting that you, and all you are and will be, *will* get to the other side of sad…and that when it seems as though everything is falling apart, it may be that because of your courage everything is actually falling into place.

– 8 –

Anxiety

The Nemesis of All Awesomeness

Need to Know (and Believe)

- Everything about fear is primal. There's no logic involved.

- If we focus all of our energy on curbing tantrums or meltdowns without addressing the cause of our anxiety, nothing will change.

- Every person on the HUMAN spectrum must LEARN to:

  ° RECOGNIZE her needs

  ° TALK to herself

  ° ASK FOR what she needs

  ° IDENTIFY and CHOOSE a solution

  ° ACCESS that solution independently.

The year was 1982. Ronald Reagan was in office. "Don't You Want Me, Baby?" was on the radio. And the smiley-face emoticon was born. But, like, what I most clearly remember about, like, that year isn't valley-girl speech or, like, Ms. PacMan. It's E.T., the Reese's-pieces-eating alien who I was absolutely sure was hiding in my closet.

Try as they might to counter my certainty that there was not, in fact, an extraterrestrial lurking in my bedroom, my parents couldn't convince me otherwise. So I clutched my teddy bear for reassurance and sat there in my bed—scared. Now, I'm not talking nervous or "trying to sneak into bed with mom and dad" scared. No, I mean to the pit of my stomach, cold sweat, freak-out-if-you-touch-me terrified.

I'd venture that most everyone reading this has felt that kind of fear at some point in her life. But try this for me: allow your body, not just your mind, to remember that feeling—your heart thudding, mind racing, stomach lurching, your little self ready to run or fight against any shadow. That's what fear actually is, you see. It's not a concept or idea, it's not a topic to be discussed rationally. Everything about fear is primal…irrational…and bodily. There's no logic involved.

Anxiety is a little bit different. Imagine the volume of that fear being turned down just a bit so that's it's not so immediate a threat or so acute a danger. Instead, it's replaced by a gnawing, jittery, ever-present sensation of *waiting* for the threat…waiting for the fear. It's like living with the *Jaws* music playing. You don't see the danger, but you surely know there's something "out there." That's anxiety.

We spectrumites, whose bodies and minds are wired a little differently, live with varying levels and intensities of almost perpetual anxiety.

That may sound paranoid, but it's not. Paranoia is irrational fear. Most of us have been bullied, are constantly assaulted by sensory input, must fend our way through daily social situations which seem random and chaotic—and often, just as we think we are at the top of our game, the rug is about to be pulled out from under us. In other words, **our anxiety is an absolutely rational reaction to the experiences we have had**.

If we focus all of our energy on curbing tantrums or meltdowns, obsessions or rigidity, we're only tearing at the leaves. Nothing will change—either in our behavior or in our hearts. It's like yanking at a weed and just tearing off the leaves. The weed disappears from view, but it isn't gone. In time, it just grows back.

But grab that weed near the base—dig at the roots and pull gently—and what happens? Yes, another weed may grow elsewhere, but this one is gone. Anxiety is that root. It is the seed from which our topical fixations and "overly sensitive," routine-driven, black-and-white obsessive behaviors arise.

We are trying to catch the rain. We are trying to create predictable order in a chaotic, often random world…by asking a million questions, by challenging exceptions to rules, by scripting dialogue we know was funny (once), or dictating play. It's not that we want to be unlikeable or difficult or dominate the conversation with topics other people don't enjoy. We just want to feel secure, safe—and to be able to stop the endless waiting for unwelcome surprises.

We've Got This, Ladies

As a child, you learned to recognize (and now, hopefully you respond) to the physical symptoms of hunger, thirst, and fatigue. That's a start toward stress-busting ninja status. But there's more, girls. Our minds are wired differently. The result is that we're more sensitive to some of what our bodies take in from the world around us (maybe sounds or smells), yet we crave other kinds of sensory input (pressure, extreme flavors/temperatures). And, just like mixed-up signals in the inner ear can cause carsickness (which seems pretty disconnected), if the sensory input we get isn't what we need, it's good bet that anxiety spikes (nervousness, stress, snappiness, confusion, etc.) will be along for the ride, too. For us, girls, independence means more than knowing how to make yourself dinner or pay your bills. It means learning to listen to our bodies and minds, manage stress and anxiety, and spend our energy on LIVING.

Every girl on the HUMAN spectrum must LEARN to:

- RECOGNIZE her needs

- TALK to herself

- ASK FOR what she needs

- IDENTIFY and CHOOSE a solution

- ACCESS that solution independently.

When I was little, I remember being taken shoe shopping by my fashion-conscious (and rather stern) grandmother. Two hours later, we left—without any shoes. I was in tears and my grandma was mortified. Every pair I'd tried had wrought a different complaint, and while I was merely being honest and trying not to waste her generosity on shoes that I wouldn't wear, she and the salesman perceived my "oversensitivity" as bratty lack of gratitude.

My mom reports that Halloween wasn't much better—*every* year. Itchy costumes made me miserable (her too, I'm sure). Trips to the beach were itchy and sandy. And heaven forbid there was an uncut (or poorly cut out) tag in my shirt or shorts...there was nothing else on earth I could think about. But back then, there was no "sensory processing disorder" or "Asperger's" label for bright, articulate children. Everyone simply decided I was a rude, overdramatic hypochondriac who couldn't play well with others.

In truth, I was a child in real pain with no one to believe me and largely without friends…but desperately in want of them. Often, our biggest hurdles come from the neurotypical adults who just don't "get how real *our* reality is." To put it bluntly, their "normalcy" is getting in the way! After all, even the best teacher or most loving parent would never think to teach us to "scratch" an "itch" that she's never felt. No one has to teach parents to understand our hunger or weariness or thirst. When a baby cries, those are the natural go-to's. Parents expect those problems, asking, "Are you hungry?", teaching both sensation recognition and vocabulary as they do. But no typical mom says, "Aw, sweetie, are you feeling dysregulated?" Instead, neurotypical adults just see raw, "bad" behavior—the symptoms of sensory/emotional dysregulation, not of bad parenting or a bad child.

On the other hand, as an Aspie adult, the idea of "overstimulation" is utterly natural. I never could make sense of people who would jangle things at my children or toss them around to try to stop their crying. If I were a baby, I'd be terrified! And, more often than not, my kids were only made more upset by the additional sensory distress well-meaning adults put "in their faces." Instead of lights and keys and gizmos, my Asperkids needed deep pressure, rhythmic motion, and white noise. As an (albeit undiagnosed) Aspie, I sensed that.

The Five Step Strategy: From Shaky to Shake-it-Up
STEP 1: RECOGNIZE WHAT YOUR BODY IS SAYING

I can't overstate this: When we feel either understimulated or overstimulated, we physically CANNOT reason, listen, or think about anything else. We can't learn. We can't rationalize well. We can't hear others' needs. It's like trying to see your own reflection in a pot of boiling water. Nothing is clear. So first thing's first: You have to learn to recognize the signs of your own sensory dysregulation (which changes from day to day and situation to situation). Remember that we can't expect others to do for us what we aren't willing to try to do for ourselves.

When sensory input is a problem, try tuning out by turning your other senses into a solution. Consider: Do I want *something to TOUCH* (stress ball, emery board, plush animal), *something to HEAR* (meditation podcast, wind chimes, sound machine), *something to SEE* (snow globe, lava lamp), *something to TASTE* (minty gum, sour candy, or even a lemon fruit leather), *something to SMELL* (candles, perfume, fresh laundry)?

STEP 2: TALK TO YOURSELF (Seriously)

Breathe slowly. Smell the roses (inhale through your nose), blow out the candles (exhale completely out of your mouth). Again. Breathe. You're going to be OK. You've felt this before—these feelings you have right now. Uncomfortable. Anxious. Embarrassed. Afraid. You've felt them, and you *have* survived. Breathe, and know you will survive this, too, wiser and stronger. The feelings can't break you. They can hurt. They can sting. They can way-lay your plans. But if you sit with the feelings—notice them, stay with them without trying to run—if you *do* sit with them and really feel them—you'll discover they have a bottom. They have an end. They aren't all-consuming. You won't drown in them. They will become shallower…eventually, shallow enough that you will begin to walk again. Keep breathing. Keep moving. Soon, you'll emerge from the hurt. You'll be able to turn around and see the far shore where you started. You'll know that you made it through and that you are powerful and resilient enough to float above anything. Right now, that sounds impossible. It feels unbearable. I know. So for now, just breathe. There is a bottom and an end. You will get there. One breath at a time. This moment will pass. It *will* be over. And you *won't* be.

Think of yourself as a detective; it's your job to figure out what your body needs.

~ Chloe Rothschild

STEP 3: ASK FOR WHAT YOU NEED.
(People Can't Read Our Minds or Bodies.)

I know—I mean really, I *know*—how hard it is to experience strong emotions *and* explain whatever it is that you're feeling. I tell neurotypicals it's a bit like being famished and having to listen to a lesson on fractions. Or having desperately to use the restroom and explain Shakespeare. Yeah, right. That's going to go well.

And really, it's awfully tough to even realize that whatever we're experiencing is different from what other people feel. Your body's normal *is your normal.* Until you use this simple process, your particular sensory needs are going to feel invisible—obviously— to you AND to everyone else. To you, they are always-been, always-known physical experiences. So, find a CALM moment and try this:

Trace this outline:

Circle or color or describe what it FEELS LIKE inside your body when others see those "outside the body" behaviors listed above. Use crayons, magazine clippings, or even a thesaurus.

Need some suggestions? Visually, black circles around your eyes could indicate tunnel vision. Squiggly lines in the legs might represent anxiety. A green swirl in the belly might be nausea. Or use words like sweaty, tight, claustrophobic, shaky.

This is BIG, important stuff, my friends. **With information— with awareness—comes POWER.** Years ago, you were taught that a rumbling, empty sensation meant you were hungry. Next, you learned that just because you felt that tummy growl, relief wasn't simply going to appear. Nope. You needed to ask for or go get food. Well, now you are both teacher *and* student. You are teaching yourself to pay attention to and identify your own biological experiences, and that's the first step toward independence. Fidgeting, squirming, thrashing—many of the negative behaviors the world associates with our kids—are really just "bigger" versions of a grumbly tummy. The body is communicating loudly—not asking for food but for protection from, or more of, the sensory input the brain needs. Once you can discern your body's messages, you can also learn to express discomfort and request whatever you need to feel better.

STEP 4: IDENTIFY AND CHOOSE A SOLUTION

Katniss Everdeen wouldn't want to enter the arena with one arrow in her quiver. And Harry Potter needed to know more than "Reducto!" to survive. No one sensory solution will always work for you *or* always be available, so like Katniss and Harry, you need options to give your body what it needs. Here are some great ones:

- chewing gum (two sticks at a time)

- "fidgets," kooshes, and stress balls

- salty pretzel rods

- sugar-free hard candies

- drinks (especially thick, cold smoothies) through a straw

- long walks or runs (repetitive motion)

- swimming

- lava lamps

- noise-canceling headphones

- swings, hammocks, gliders (include back and forth AND in circles going both directions)

- rocking chairs

- beanbag chairs

- a calming room where you can be alone

- Irlen-colored lenses for glasses (reduces visual fatigue)

- climbing (trees or indoor wall/mountain climbing)

- pounding (clay, play dough, hammer/nails)

- spinning (twisted swing, office chair)

- playing catch with a weighted ball or heavy pillow

- human burrito (swaddle yourself in a blanket and roll back and forth)

- hot showers or baths

- classical music

- meditation podcasts

- locks, keys, and switches

- tug-of-war with a table leg and a stretchy exercise band

- yoga

- scented candles

- massage

STEP 5: ACCESS A SOLUTION

Asperger's, autism, attention deficit disorder/attention deficit hyperactivity disorder, and/or sensory processing disorder are real, MEDICAL diagnoses. Therefore, you have the right to expect easy, independent access to whatever tools you need—regardless of what rules apply to other pupils. You are not asking for favors. By occupying your nerves as your body needs, you create a sense of balance—that means better focus, more emotional calm, and deeper concentration. You're stating what you need. (After all, is it special treatment that someone who is nearsighted gets to wear her contacts to school?)

Experiment with various sensory strategies and assemble your favorites into a toolkit; keep kits in your desk, locker, room, school counselor's office, and/or your car.

Share your needs (privately) with teachers and supervisors BEFORE you have a tough time, so they can work *with* you and empower you.

Create a plan for "escape" to a quiet place (the library, a counselor's office, etc.) when emotions get too overwhelming. You should be able to excuse yourself without making your needs public knowledge.

Doing It Anyway

There was no alien in my bedroom back in 1982, of course. But in my thirty-odd years of life, I've met very real danger in places and with people that should have been as familiar and safe as a childhood haven. Those of us on the spectrum want to be liked, want to please—even to impress. We certainly don't want to *be* the problem.

If you can remember that in the hardest moments, if you can remember what the feeling of true fear is, then you can give yourself a great gift: respect, understanding, and a plan.

After all, courage is feeling fear and doing the "scary stuff" anyway. Those of us on the spectrum have to choose to be courageous almost every day. Like that little girl in the bedroom back in 1982, when we *are* afraid (even if that fear is unnecessary), we certainly don't want to feel condescended to or be punished. We need understanding, respect, and patience. Like I did years ago (and still do now), we all need allies—stuffed or otherwise—to cling to until we can steady ourselves…until we can see, peeking through the fear, the safety and calm of an unsullied tomorrow.

Something Special

The Box on the Shelf

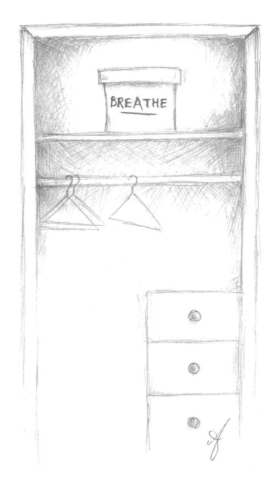

Your mind is racing. And now, no matter how hard you try, no matter how many people tell you to lay off or tone it down, no matter how much you hear "Don't worry about it," you just can't stop thinking.

That thing that might happen. Or that might not happen. There are other things you have to do. Other things you *want* to do. But dang it, you're stuck in endless loops of "yeah but, what if…?"

"Just don't think about it," they say. And all you can think is, "Oh. OK. Thanks. There's one I hadn't tried."

"Let it go," the song says. But you shake your head. And pick at your cuticles. If only letting go were as easy as Disney makes it sound.

I know. I get it. You're exhausted. You're alone in your head. And you need some help getting out.

Here's how we're going to make that happen: Imagine that you are holding a box. It has a lid, which you take off and put aside. Now imagine that thing you're worried about. Maybe you see a photograph of it. Maybe you picture words on scraps of paper. Maybe you see a movie clip. It doesn't matter how you envision the worry. It's your idea and your box. So however you do it, you're doing it right.

Next, see yourself placing the worry into the box, and put the lid back on. Although the sides are opaque (you can't see through), you know what's in there, and you know it's safe.

Next, imagine that you write one word on one side of the box: "BREATHE." Because it's really enough if that's as much as you can do. Really.

Now envision an empty closet. There's no door—you can see the shelves clearly. Place the box on one of those shelves, with the "BREATHE" side facing out. Step away.

Your worry is there. It's safe. No one can take it away from you, and if you need to go back and check on it at some point, you can. It'll still be there. You don't have to let it go. But you do get to take a break.

What will you do now? Well, you can also walk away for a little bit. The length of time—a minute or a month—isn't important. What matters is that you are in charge now. So, take it down and look when you need to look. Leave it there if you feel like you can. Or just glance up, read…and BREATHE. Safely. Steadily.

You've got it. It just no longer has *you*.

9

You Cannot Actually Die of Embarrassment

Happily, you cannot ACTUALLY
die of embarrassment.

I know.
I AM the lab rat.

Need to Know (and Believe)

- When we are keyed up emotionally—maybe angry or frustrated, nervous, worried, even giddy or excited—we are much more likely to do and say things impulsively.

- Planning is power.

- Notepads are a great way to "let it out" without actually letting it out.

- Always remember HALT (hungry, angry, lonely, tired).

We've all been there. Trying to scoop our words up off of the floor—to reel them back in. I call it "watermelon syndrome." And I, too, have suffered.

In 1987, a movie called *Dirty Dancing* came out, and although I was little at the time, I'm pretty sure that, over the years, I've seen it more than twenty-three times. The whole story is basically about a goody-two-shoes girl who falls in love with the "bad boy" dance instructor at a summer getaway. As both a goody-two-shoes *and* a dancer, I was all over this thing.

This many years later, I think I still have almost every line memorized—but my favorite isn't some perfectly timed zinger or swoon-worthy whisper. Nope. What I love most is what Goody-Two-Shoes Girl manages to say when she finally has the chance to speak to Mr. Hot Stuff.

Scene: secret party (and therefore infinitely cooler than any she's ever been to). Wild music (she is utterly *not* wild). Over-the-top dancing (she can't dance to save her life). Then, Johnny notices her. This is a social once-in-a-lifetime moment—maybe.

"What is *she* doing here?" he asks with disdain.

And in a moment of total cringe worthiness, she answers, "I carried a watermelon."

Yep. That's it. She toted fruit. He rolls his eyes, walks away, and instantly, she wants to die of utter uncoolness. "I carried a WATERMELON?!" she yells, slamming her forehead against the wall. Errgh!

Everyone at some point or another says the perfectly wrong thing at the perfectly wrong time. My advanced-placement U.S. history teacher began our year by telling the sophomores in the room that she didn't think we had any business being there. "This class is simply too demanding," she warned. To which I retorted, "Just watch us." OUT LOUD. (Even today, the surest way to get me to do something is to tell me I can't. "Just watch me!" I still say. Only now I know and only say it to *myself.*)

Here's another doozy: While I was on a first date years ago, it happened to come up in conversation that my mom was undergoing treatment for breast cancer. "Really?" the guy nodded, trying to make small talk. "Yeah, my aunt died of that."

What??? Hey, I know he was just nervous; he wasn't trying to be rude. But if ever there was an example of "You don't actually have to say everything that pops into your head," there you have it.

Here's the takeaway: **When we are keyed up emotionally— maybe angry or frustrated, nervous, worried, even giddy or excited—we are much more likely to do and say things impulsively, without thinking about the circumstances or the effects. And the results are usually not stellar.**

Let me paint a picture: Say there's a domino run set up on the floor of a hallway. If you are distracted by an annoying tag or flickering light, you don't quite feel like you belong (like Goody-Two-Shoes Girl), or you feel pressured to make witty conversation (my date), you're probably not going to pay steady attention to those dominoes. Odds are, you're going to accidentally knock one down, which is going to knock *all* of the rest down, too. That's like social fallout—the unintended consequences or friendly fire of speaking impulsively.

Things get messy fast. There are, however, a few tips I've learned along the way to prevent watermelon syndrome:

- **Planning is power.** Pay attention to which people or situations trigger you. Then, when you know similar circumstances are ahead, problem solve ahead of time.

- **Recall a cringe-worthy situation** and ask yourself what you thought, what you felt (an adjective), how your body felt (nauseous, sweaty, dizzy, etc.), and what you did. The next time you start to recognize those signs, spend five minutes calming down. Take some deep breaths, and consciously choose your next steps based on what you *want to happen*— not on how you were feeling a few minutes ago.

- **Notepads (both real and on your phone) are awesome.** If you notice that you frequently blurt things out because you're afraid you'll forget your ideas, *write them out!* You can even text yourself if you need to satisfy the urge to act immediately (I have!). Do not be embarrassed by needing to jot down your thoughts. Why do you think every phone and tablet comes with reminder and to-do features?

- Being **(H)ungry, (A)ngry, (L)onely, or (T)ired** (remember HALT) clouds thinking, often leading to decisions or comments you'll regret. Try to arm yourself by eating a healthy snack and exercising. Go for a walk while listening to a meditation podcast, an audiobook, or your favorite music. Or toss in "Just Dance 2014." Ride a bike. Swim some laps. Whatever you like to do, do it. Physical work calms your nervous system; it's sweaty, but it's true.

Undoing the "Doh!"

What if you've already "watermelon'ed"? Don't freak. Every one of us has memories that embarrass us. Every one of us feels less than fabulous about something. You know…those choices that may not have served you too well, the not-so-flattering ways others perceive you, the "good enough isn't really good enough" imperfections that gnaw away at your gut…

Like a filmy residue, shame sticks to your soul, and before long, it actually feels familiar. It feels right. And since it's not going anywhere, we have to find a way of dealing (or not dealing) with our shame—and usually that comes in the form of self-punishment. We seek out what we think we deserve in hurtful relationships. We cut ourselves. We starve ourselves. We stuff ourselves. Or we try to get numb to it all.

So, let's take the sting out of "Doh!" moments. Let's benefit from constructive feedback. Here's all you have to do:

1. Picture a chalkboard

2. Imagine your "whoops" moment/critical feedback is either named in writing or sketched as a cartoony doodle.

3. Notice—you are not made of chalk. YOU are not on the Board. The "Thing" is separate from you. The choices, blunders, and misunderstandings others didn't like *exist apart from you. They aren't you.*

4. Now, face 'em without flinching. Without looking away. I know, it may feel uncomfortable *now.* But *now* doesn't last long. And if you don't deal with the pesky "Things," they shape-shift…they become shame.

In 1985, tabloid magazines published nude pictures of Madonna that had been taken when she was a struggling artist's model. Suddenly, those photos were global. It would have been easy, don't you think, for Madonna to hide in shame…to hang her head in humiliation? But she didn't. She took ownership of the situation and spoke back to the scandal and collaborated with two of the decade's biggest artists, Andy Warhol and Keith Haring, to make art and headlines of her own. Above a smiling photo, she used three words, simple and to the point, to bravely self-talk in public…the same three I want you to repeat as often as necessary: "I'm not ashamed."

The more you know yourself,
the more power there is in your
authenticity.

~Brigid Rankowski

The first time I met my husband, I was at work. He'd been watching me and was totally embarrassed when I looked over and noticed. To try to save face, he turned and quickly began studying a nearby bulletin board (very seriously). Though I couldn't see it, I happened to know that this particular board was completely empty. "See anything interesting?" I teased.

Now, that could've easily become a watermelon syndrome moment for him, but he did something simple and genuine—and it worked. Instead of trying to cover up his blunder or cracking a joke, he smiled shyly, faced me, and extended his right hand. "Hi," he said. "I'm John." That was it. And that was all it took. You see, you don't have to be smooth or slick. In the end, you just have to be *yourself*. (Watermelon not required.)

10

Blanching at Perfectionism

Real Girls Aren't Perfect. And Perfect Girls Aren't Real.

Need to Know (and Believe)

- Other people don't like you more if, by expecting more of yourself, you make them feel less.

- Whomever you're worried about impressing isn't paying all that much attention to what you do or don't do flawlessly. They're thinking about themselves.

- Perfectionism is the highest form of self-harm. You'll *never* feel perfect, but you *will* always feel like a failure.

- You are not a done deal.

- On those days when you truly can't say anything nice about yourself—practice.

The Golden Girls was a hit sitcom during the 1980s, years when my Saturday nights were filled with babysitters and television I don't think I was actually allowed to watch. The show was about four not-so-young-but-way-too-lively-to-be-over-the-hill gals who become housemates…and then typical comedy hijinks ensue. Blanche, a former southern belle, was the vamp of the bunch. She was used to men's attention and unapologetically enjoyed their affections as much as they enjoyed hers, delightedly continuing that Scarlett O'Hara role into her "golden" years.

In one episode (which obviously must've affected me as I still remember it), an unexpected snafu upset Blanche's typical finesse. She'd met and fallen quite hard for a devastatingly handsome man who was equally taken with her. So what, her friends wondered, was wrong? Why did she seem so very nervous and agitated? The problem was this: her beau was blind, and Blanche could not imagine how on earth she would keep the attention of a man who couldn't see her. Her looks, her body language, her come-hither charm were what she was "good at." Without those, what did she have to offer?

Like many of us, Blanche valued herself based upon what had, in the past, brought her acceptance, approval, and a sense of worth.

Perfection is just an illusion.
And you can do better magic than that.

~ Anne-Louise Richards

Everyone wants to feel like a success. And we, on the spectrum, have often had more than our fair share of unexpected "mess-ups," leading to more than our fair share of teasing, rejection, and insults. It's not really too surprising that, if we are told we "are" something special—smart, talented, creative—then maintaining that identity holds a great sway over our self-esteem. So, in all the trying to keep up appearances, we feel perpetually anxious that we'll make a mistake and lose whatever it is about ourselves that has *finally* garnered approval. Like Blanche, **take away our "something special" and we're sure that we are suddenly nothing at all**. We beat ourselves up for being imperfect when in fact, trying to be perfect is the most imperfect goal imaginable. It's not achievable. It doesn't exist. So we end up utterly terrified that we'll "look stupid," be laughed at, be called out as "posers" or frauds—not really as good as the world had thought. **We feel** we have to be better or more special than everyone else around us. Basically, **we have to be better than human.** Like Blanche, **we attach our value to our performance rather than to our personhood.** We become bullies—of ourselves.

Ability, Confidence, and Mismatch

No secret here. Your most vicious critic is the voice inside your own head. Hear her? She'll repeat whatever she picks up in the big, bad world. "You're not smart enough," she'll say. "You're so annoying. You're weird. You're depressing." Know what? Not only is that girl mean—she's wrong. It's a fact: the world throws loads of obstacles in the path of every girl. Please. Please. *Please* don't allow yourself to become yet *another* something in your own way.

> To become successful, try different things,
> go to different places, ask a lot of questions.
> You may fail, but you will also learn new
> things from each experience.
>
> ~ Robyn Steward

Some years ago, psychologist Carol Dweck took a good, hard look at a bunch of very bright fifth-grade boys and girls. Specifically, she observed what happened when these kids were presented with new concepts—confusing information meant to cause them a bit of frustration. How, Dr. Dweck wondered, would they handle the stress?

Among the girls in the study, the higher the IQ, the *more likely they were to give up* when asked to learn something that was particularly foreign or complex. That's right: **the *most* intelligent girls didn't stick around and keep thinking**. They didn't persevere. They quit. Fast. And there's more bad news. The girls with perfect grades—straight A's—reported the most intense feelings of helplessness of any kids in the entire study. On the other hand, boys in the very same group saw the very same difficult material as challenging, even energizing. **Instead of giving up, the boys were far more likely to increase their focus and turn up the effort.**

When I read about this study, it made me heartsick. Why would that happen? The girls should've been the most confident kids in the room. The most resilient. The ones who said, "Let me at it!" At fifth-grade testing levels, there is a consistent standard: girls routinely outscore boys in *every* subject, *including* math and science (whoever said those weren't "girl subjects?!"). So the trouble couldn't be a matter of intelligence *or* classroom success. **The only difference between the boys and girls was how they reacted to difficulty—to the possibility of not having the ready answer, of pleasing everyone, of shining brightly.** When the going got tough, the girls got going. As in out the door. Gone. **These clever young girls turned on themselves as if they'd been waiting for proof of being not good enough.** In mere minutes, they'd lost all confidence and walked away in shame.

Now, I'm being honest. The single best motivator for me has *always* been when I'm told that I can't do something. "Oh really?" I think. "Just watch me—and watch me do it better than you ever could!" So, I would LOVE to tell you that I'd never fall for such silly mind games—love to say I could never be so easily undone. I'd love to tell you that. But the truth is, I'd be lying if I did.

My best friend from high school once said, "When we were little kids, I knew two things about Jenny Cook: she had red hair, and she was really, really smart." Those were my only for-sures. My identity, as far as I could count on it. And from the outside looking in, neither bullet point varied through the years. By the time I was in university, I had a perfect grade point average, would be graduating with honors, and was known on campus as "the redhead" (though I'm pretty sure now that being known by anything but my own name wasn't really the compliment I saw it to be). Identity in tact. Or so it seemed. On the inside, I was swirling out of control, totally disconnected from the person I'd always been.

Why? Well, my boyfriend of almost two years—with whom I was absolutely head-over-heels—had pointed out that all of my classes were in the humanities. He was in the sciences and had not done nearly as well at school, despite being every bit as smart. So, he told me, I was obviously outperforming him because my classes were much easier. I was a fraud, an arrogant pretense... as well as a lot of other bad things, he explained. Many times. **And because I loved him, I believed him. I just no longer believed in myself.**

In a nutshell, **when something is truly difficult, bright, talented, creative girls often interpret their struggle as proof that they just don't have what it takes**. That whatever smartness, cleverness, and goodness they have (or don't have) is inborn. Unchangeable. Innate. Part of an "either-you've-got-it-or-you-don't" package. And being on the spectrum adds a whole extra dimension to that concept. By our very nature, we tend to see the world in acute all-or-nothing, I've-got-this-or-I'm-an-utter-failure terms anyway. **Bright girls, in general, are likely to see themselves as inadequate—and spectrum girls add an extra dose of intensity, anxiety, depression, and self-loathing.** As soon as life experiences "prove" our shortcomings, our worst fears are realized. The smart (or creative or imaginative) person we thought we knew—well, she's turned out to be a scam, after all. Turns out we *are* fakes. Frauds. And really, why keep at what you obviously can't do well when you can, to some gratification, focus your ultrafierce attentions on the one person who deserves your scorn for being such a failure? Yourself.

Super-Important, Cannot-Possibly-Be-Overstated Fact

I'm now gonna tell it like it is because certain deadly, dangerous, disfiguring specters haunt girls on the spectrum more than any other population: eating disorders and self-mutilation (such as intentionally cutting or burning ourselves). It makes sense if you just think about it; genetically, we are prime candidates. We're socially programmed to judge ourselves harshly. We're neurologically wired to be rigid and exacting, to be perfectionists with obsessive and depressive tendencies, to have minds that get stuck on something and replay the idea endlessly all day and night. And we don't like to feel out of control. We are, literally, the textbook illustration of the kind of girl/woman most vulnerable to self-harm.

Let's be clear. You deserve love. And understanding. And compassion. You are not a mistake, my friend. You are not some amoral piece of garbage who'd do better to numb out and disappear. You are good at much more than destroying yourself. Do you hear me? Losing yet another pound, hiding one more scar, stuffing down one more cookie—it isn't a triumph. It doesn't make you superior to anyone, even though I know that's how it can feel.

Years ago, I was hospitalized for anorexia and, on some, deeply troubled level, I was actually proud of the "achievement." Really. Proud of getting so good at losing weight, at being so skinny—in reality, so malnourished—that I had to be admitted to a hospital for a month. And you know what? The day before I went inpatient, I was still getting compliments on my uber-teeny jeans. So, I didn't really want "recovery"—to lose my only coping mechanism. I felt light and numb and admired…until I was admitted and finally discovered that no, I was just wholly sick—and wholly friendless. You see, after a while, you begin to love your addiction.

Cutting. Starving. Compulsive exercising. Drinking. Drugs. All of it is about relief. But you know what? You don't get away. And the relief is only temporary. What really happens is this: you get ashamed and secretive and ever more isolated. Then, finally, when you emerge from the fog—*if* you emerge—life won't have magically turned around. You're not a monster, and you're not invisible. You're just imperfect. And now, you'll also find that you are very, very sick.

What I Ask of You

1. Do *not* say "I'm fine" when you're not. No matter how alone you feel—no matter how to-blame you believe you are… you aren't. I'm telling you this from personal experience, my friend. You deserve—you need—*real* people in your life who aren't afraid of sadness. Real people—parents, siblings, counselors, teachers—who will come closer when you cry. Who will put a hand softly on your shoulder or wrap you in a hug and say, "No, you're not. And I'm still not leaving."

2. Instead of hurting yourself, try one of the alternatives on the next page. Self-harm isn't about attention seeking. It's about control. The reality is that there are a lot more things in life which we can't control than those we can. You can't engineer every conversation or job or date or class. But you can be 100% in charge of *how* you respond to your triggers.

Self-harm alternatives			
Ask for a hug.	Write a poem.	Draw butterflies in marker on your skin.	Do yoga.
Color in a coloring book.	Watch your favorite cartoon rerun.	Explore Pinterest.	Crunch ice.
Go for a walk.	Take a bubble bath.	Make a calming jar.	Run your hands under really cold water.
Cry.	Plant flowers.	Do a crossword puzzle.	Learn to swear in another language.
Yell. LOUD.	Eat a popsicle.	Take a nap.	Jump on a trampoline.
Play with an animal.	Play with Play-Doh.	Reorganize a closet.	Finger-paint to music.
Blow bubbles.	Do a puzzle.	Edit photos.	Dance.
Drive with the windows open and music on.	Bake brownies.	Feel your pulse.	Watch your favorite film.
Punch a pillow.	Close your eyes and focus on your breathing.	Clap your hands hard.	Tear newspaper.
Throw ice cubes at a wall until they shatter.	Pour rice, beans, or ice water into a bowl and submerge your hands. Let it run through your fingers.	Draw patterns on your skin.	Say "I am worthy of love" 20 times out loud in a mirror.

Don't Play It Safe

How often have you found yourself avoiding challenges (in schoolwork, favorite activities, trying—or not—to make friends) or choosing goals that you knew would be easy for you to reach? Are there things you decided—without trying or without trying for long—that you could never be good at? Skills you believed you could never really make your own? If you're nodding or thinking, "Oh geez, well, yeah, actually"—then deep down you believe that you are "stuck." That you will be exactly who and what you are now—forever. Inadequate. Left out. A burden. And that conviction is determining more of the course of your life than you've probably ever imagined. Which would be fine if your abilities *were* innate and unchangeable. Only they're not.

You are not a done deal. You are malleable. Moldable and changeable. Sure, everyone has certain aptitudes and talents. Not everyone will be Ada Lovelace or Sally Ride or Marie Curie. Which is a good thing. The world needs Emily Dickinsons and Jane Austens and Jane Goodalls, too…and it needs *you*. So give yourself a little more credit. On those days when you truly can't say anything nice about yourself—practice. As the expression goes, Mother Teresa didn't walk around worrying about the size of her thighs or the last thing she'd said—she had *stuff to do*. So do you. Get going.

Maybe you think you're not quite ready to put yourself out there, to step outside of your comfort zone. Want to know the truth? You're never really *ready* and perfectionism is the mother of procrastination. Stop worrying about looking "stupid." The truth is that whomever you're worried about impressing isn't paying all that much attention to what you do or don't do flawlessly. They're thinking about themselves. Just like you are right now.

So stop making seven thousand excuses and explanations and rationalizations (you know…that it's-safer-if-I-stay-in-my-head-away-from-my-heart thing we're sooo good at?) about why you can't or shouldn't or won't, and TRY something that scares you. Push your boundaries. Learn a new language. Try a drawing class. Learn photography. Drink chocolate milk instead of white milk. Who cares how big or small—just get going. Being alive is about taking risks. Sometimes you'll amaze yourself with unknown talents. Other times, not so much. So what? You just proved you were brave. And THAT's worth discovering.

In fact—and don't take this the wrong way—I hope things don't turn out neat and pretty and expected and right all the time. Make messes, sing off-key, drop things, goof up. That's what happens when you push boundaries and ask questions…when you start to change the world just by being yourself.

Girls, your resilience, your self-control, your charm, your athleticism—every ability and every skill *will change* based on life experience, intensity of effort, creativity of approach, and good old-fashioned stick-to-itiveness. Remember, EVERYTHING is hard before it's easy. Everything. So grab on tightly to the fact that you can *always* improve. That ability *isn't* an either/or, now or never. Go out there, girls, and take this life for every wild, boisterous, jubilant minute you've got.

Spectrum kids need to prove
to the world they can do great things.

~ Temple Grandin

Arrogantly Insecure

You and I know that perfectionism isn't about being precise or meticulous. It's a measure of great insecurity. Of fear. Of "what if's" gone haywire: what if I make a mistake...what if I let everyone down...what if they all laugh at me...what if I ruin everything...what if I'm not good enough? Yeah. Really. What if? The world will not end, I promise. And you cannot actually die of embarrassment. I know. I'm the lab rat.

The ironic thing is that **perfectionism comes off as arrogance**, which is not going make people invite you to sit at their lunch tables. In my own life as "perfect girl," I see now that I inadvertently sent the condescending message that I believed myself superior to everyone else. Maybe I felt afraid or disappointed in myself, but from any other person's perspective, I was insulting them. I made other people feel lousy about themselves, then jealous of, and completely irritated by, me. Meaning, of course, that they would treat me as if I were vain and self-centered. Which, not meaning to be, I guess I was.

"The Perfect Rule" is one of the very *first* topics covered in *The Asperkid's (Secret) Book of Social Rules: The Handbook of Not-So-Obvious Social Guidelines*, because it's a big issue. And a surmountable one, if you know these things:

- Perfectionism is the highest form of self-harm. You'll *never* feel perfect, but you *will* always feel like a failure.

- You are *not* a "one-trick pony." You have many talents, most of which you've not even discovered yet—and every one of which is essential to someone.

- Who you are is far more important than what you do.

- Watch your own words. Criticizing others' weight, appearance, intelligence, etc., reinforces the message, "I won't like you as much, either, if you fall short of the mark."

In thirty-something years, I've learned that **other people don't like you more if, by expecting more of yourself, you make**

them feel less. Instead, the way to earn *real* respect and inclusion is by learning to be relatably *imperfect*. When you mess up, bobble, wobble, and keep on going (maybe even with a chuckle!), *you don't look stupid, you look human*—and that's "golden" news to *any* girl, *anywhere* on the human spectrum.

Special Stuff

Daisy's Lesson

This is my dog, Daisy. She's not the smartest dog I've ever loved, but she does know one thing that a lot of people don't. Daisy's favorite part of the day is riding in the car when I drive the kids to school. And, like most dogs, she loves sticking her nose out of the open window to sniff the breeze. In fact, she loves it so much that she has even figured out how to open the window all by herself…with a little "dogged" perseverence.

But one day, there was a change in her routine. Our car was in the shop for some repair work, so we made the morning trip in a rental car. And this time, when Daisy stepped on what she expected to be the window control, nothing happened. She sniffed curiously at the glass. Nothing. That window was not opening.

Now, do you think Daisy got frustrated and then maybe angry at somebody else? Did she bark at herself? Did she howl? Did she lay down and decide all was lost—that it just wasn't worth the effort anymore? No. **She just tried something different.** She moved her paw around a few times, pressing and sniffing, and finally, landed right on the control button. Voila! Open window. Happy dog.

The next time you feel like you've "messed up," remember Daisy and her window. *Whatever isn't working isn't a mistake. It's a message. Look closely. Be patient. Stick with it, and try something a little different.*

Daisy knows you can do it. And so do I.

Quotealicious

- 11 -

Sexuality

The Venn Diagram They Didn't Teach in School

Need to Know (and Believe)

- You are not empty or blank. You are a person with power, rights, and wants, even if you're not yet sure what they are.

- Pleasure is not a dirty word.

- Sexuality is a mix of emotional closeness, sensuality, gender and orientation, reproduction and health, active expression, freedom, and power.

In ancient Rome, kids who were fortunate enough to go to school (and by "kids" I mean "boys") used a wooden stylus to carve their notes onto a flat wax tablet. Once used, the *tabula* could easily be refreshed by reheating and smoothing the wax, leaving a *tabula rasa*, an "unscribed tablet" or "blank slate." Nowadays, *tabula rasa* is an expression used to mean a new start...a mind that is completely fresh, clear, and pure, free of outside influences, experiences, pressures, or ideas.

If you'll remember, I explained earlier that the word "autism" comes from the word for "self" ...that, yes, we have a hard time separating our wants and desires and thoughts from everyone else's. I think that's largely because, when it comes to our own identity, so many of us feel like *tabulae rasae*. We're waiting to be told what to like, whom to like, how to feel, how to act—I get that we *really* need specific guidance (I like to call them "Las Vegas neon signs") to help us navigate. But notice I said a lot of us "*feel* like" blank slates. I didn't say we actually *are* blank—we most certainly should *not* be waiting around to take orders or to do whatever is necessary to fit in. No way.

My favorite poem in the world, "Song of Myself" by Walt Whitman says, "You shall not look through my eyes either, nor take things from me. / You shall listen to all sides and filter them from yourself." *That* is precisely what I think we need to do—to listen (without interrupting), observe (without judgment), ask questions, and then let what we've learned sift through our souls. Toss out anything that makes you feel less than, unwanted, or put down. Keep whatever speaks to your heart, builds you up, and empowers you to become more of precisely who and what you are already.

We each have to learn how to be true to ourselves in every area of life—including sexuality. Because you are not a *tabula rasa*. You are not empty or blank. You are a person with power, rights, and wants, even if you're not yet sure what they are.

Acceptance of self is the key to health and happiness. My self-acceptance has made a path for my transition.

~ Zaffy Simone

So, let's start with a fundamental concept that's anything but simple: **sexuality is not the same as "sex."** Okaaayyy…what the heck is "sexuality" then? Is it your gender? Well, partly. Is it whom you find attractive? Partly. Is it what you do (or don't do) with another person? Partly. Is it even a thing if you don't really have any of "that kind" of interest in boys *or* girls? Yep. Everyone has a sexuality.

There are probably a hundred different ways to help explain the idea of "sexuality," but that's ninety-nine more than we need. So, let's go with this: **Sexuality is a mix of many different things—physical, emotional, chemical, social, intellectual, and cultural—that is unique to each person.** We've already said that to live your best life, you need to discover your truest self. Your *whole* self. And that "self" includes your sexuality. And that, girls, is why I'm telling you that, for you to live a life that is safe and happy, you need to understand your sexuality as its own thing. Its own unique recipe that is an indivisible part of you, completely independent from anyone else in the world.

Oh, and if nothing else will convince you that this is important to take your time in discovering, there's this: Do you know what people (both male and female) universally report to be the most attractive characteristic in another person? Self-confidence—the comfortable sureness that only comes from getting to really know and appreciate yourself, asking for what you want, and consistently refusing anything that lessens you. That's big stuff. And it starts here.

Personally, I'm a lover of a good illustration for making complicated ideas a little less mind-boggling. So, let's give that a try now, shall we? **Sexuality is a mix of**:

- **Sensuality**—Notice the word "sense." We're talking about your physical senses and your awareness and experience of them. Sensuality also involves our awareness and experience of our bodies as a whole, including our body image, and our experiences, if any, of physically exploring the bodies of others. Sensuality is about pleasure: seeking, exploring, and experiencing pleasure, both as something we may receive or have, and as something we may give others or share with others. **Pleasure is not a dirty word.**

- **Closeness**—You might also say intimacy, sharing, caring, emotional risk taking, and vulnerability. Emotional intimacy may not always occur with every sexual experience, and when it does, it doesn't always look or feel the same way for everyone, or with every experience—including for two people sharing a sexual experience together at the same time—nor happen to the same degree for every person or with every sexual experience. While sexual pleasure *can* exist independently, emotional closeness makes it a whole lot better.

- **Gender and Orientation**—This describes your feeling, sense, or understanding of who you are as a woman (not physically female—but what "womanly" or "girlie" means *to you)*, the ways you express those feelings to the world, and what gender of people (if any) you find attractive.

- **Health and Reproduction**—This includes the information we have about sexual anatomy, pregnancy, sexual activities, reproduction, contraception, prevention of sexually transmitted diseases, and self-care, and the values we attach to those topics. Your mental health (for example, anxiety, depression) is also a big part of your sexual health; after all, clear thinking is an essential ingredient of good decision making.

- **Active Expression**—Who is doing what when it comes to her own body parts and/or those of a sexual partner. This also includes knowing what you do *not* want to do.

- **Freedom and Power**—At the center of everything is this, the most important piece. Freedom refers to what a person has the right or ability to do. Power describes the physical and emotional control you have over your body and your sense of worth. Sometimes, it's obvious that a woman has been overpowered—that physically, another person is using her body against her will. But often, our power to negotiate, decide, agree to, or refuse sexual experiences is wrapped up in complicated emotions. That's how others can manipulate, control, or harm us—and yet we may still feel guilty.

You can be sure you are using your freedom and power in healthy ways when you:

- care for yourself and about others

- seek out mutual pleasure and well-being

- respect yourself, your decisions, your likes and dislikes, and those of others too

- accept only the same from everyone else.

- 12 -

No "Right" Way to "Be a Girl"

Need to Know (and Believe)

- Even when you try to listen to and figure out your deepest self, it can be really hard to tell which inner voice is your own.

- Some spectrum girls aren't interested in "classically girlie" things. Others are very interested. Both are completely fine. How you "do female" is yours to invent, change, rework, and be proud of, without explanation to anyone else.

- "Hot" and "beautiful" are not the same thing. Neither are "want" and "like."

- When you are up "on a pedestal," you can get knocked down fast. No one looks you in the eye as an equal when you're up there. They look at you as an object. And every object is disposable.

"Sticks and stones may break my bones, but names will never hurt me" ought to be in some kind of WRONGNESS Hall of Fame. You know…right alongside the idea that using a tampon somehow might make you not a virgin. Both are SO VERY WRONG. Not only can words hurt, they can cut you to the quick in ways that physical injuries never do. And thanks to social media, words have a permanence and a public reach that they've never had before. But even before Instagram or Facebook, words have always stung far longer than a slap or pinch.

Spoken or written, other people's words etch themselves into our souls, shaping and reshaping the ways we understand who we "actually" are. Which means that **even when you try to listen to and figure out your deepest self, it can be really hard to tell which inner voice is your own**.

That confusion can get particularly mucky when trying to understand our own sexuality—our individual ways of "being female." Recently, a young girl on the spectrum told me that she wasn't a "girly girl." I raised an eyebrow and smirked. "Really?

But aren't you a girl, Elizabeth?" She laughed and replied, "Of course!"

"Well, then," I answered her. "Anything you do *is* being a girlie girl…because you *are* a girl…so any way you choose to 'do' girl is girlie—and wonderful!"

The world seems to think that girls and women on the spectrum have no interest in "looking girlie" in the "expected" ways (such as make-up, dresses, and flirting). That is absolutely true for *some* girls. If you show up on this planet without a strong sense of "self"—of I am fill-in-the-blank—you may very well look at traditional "girl stuff" (or "boy stuff") and think, why should *that* be assigned to me? As a group, neurotypical girls do, in general, feel more driven to blend in socially.

So, yes, **it's quite possible that your spectruminess—especially the part about not really thinking about or feeling super-affected by what other people want—might actually give you the freedom to step back and question gender rules in a unique way. Which is awesome. And important. For everyone.**

That said, **other spectrum women do happily wear high heels and lip gloss. And that's OK, too.** You see, some of us are *very* eager to get classic, traditional ideas of "being girlie" right—as much as our perfectionism drives us to get everything else "right," too. Some of us enjoy "old-school glamour" because we're more comfortable "following rules"—or because we like starting with those rules, playing around with them, and then inventing our own, fresh versions of the classics. That's both smart and creative!

Spectrum girls like me are (oft-charming) mimics. We study. We copy witty expressions and learn how to perfect come-hither looks. We play characters…and sometimes, caricatures. We wear personas—not necessarily false or bad, but definitely, consciously learned. I mean, heck, when I was in college, I wrote my honors thesis on Barbie. Yep. The doll. I spent two years researching, studying, and writing a book about Barbie as a "didactic tool of postwar modern femininity in America."

Translation? I literally made an academic course out of learning the expectations of my own society and my own era. It made me feel safe…and it wasn't as though I'd checked my brain (or sass) at the door. I liked the aesthetic—and, admittedly, the easier inclusion. And that's OK, too. Again: **there is no WRONG way to be a girl—including preferring more "classic" expressions of femininity**!

The Evolution of You

How you "do female" is yours to invent, change, rework, and be proud of, without explanation to anyone else. You are free to make your own choices. You must also be responsible for your reactions to the consequences of those choices.

If you challenge the status quo, expect that you will make some people *very* uncomfortable. That's not a threat—it's a fact. When people feel confused, afraid, or uneasy, they can try to learn and grow…or they may just get mean. **It's sad, but true: some people will judge you based on what you are wearing.** They'll try to use *your* sexuality as a weapon against you. They'll call you names. They'll mix up gender identity and sexual orientation. They'll slander you, using names like "butch" or "dike." They'll repackage something beautiful as shameful, something intensely personal as a topic for public discussion.

On the flip side, you have nothing—absolutely nothing—to be ashamed of if you want boys or girls to find you "traditionally" attractive…or if they *do*. **Just know that the world isn't always kind to those who "get it too right" either.** When you "excel," others (inaccurately) may well perceive you as a threat… and suddenly, you're the target of their deepest anxieties and insecurities.

So, guess what? The lesson is that none of us can please all of the people all of the time. You have to be sure you're choosing whatever you choose because it suits YOU, not based on hoped-for approval or fear of rejection. Genuinely ask yourself: Are you choosing the ways you express "woman" because they feel comfortable and natural to you (great!)? Or because your heart is so starved for affection that sexual attention can feel "close enough"?

I'll be honest. I've done both.

In the span of one performance weekend (as the femme fatale lead in my high school musical), I literally went from having almost no social life to feeling like the honeypot surrounded by awfully hungry bees. Boys were everywhere. Calling, flirting. Walking me here or driving me there. There were party invitations every weekend. I wasn't just *not* unwanted. I was being actively sought out and fought over. For a girl used to being on the edges of things, it felt like I was Alice through the looking glass, and I did NOT want to leave. Two years later, I discovered that I'd been included on a "Top 10 Hottest Girls in the Senior Class" list. Every young woman in the school agreed that it was a totally immature, sexist prank…and every one of us on the list was also secretly—sheepishly—thrilled to be included.

Since then, I've discovered that **when you are put up on a pedestal, you can get knocked down fast. No one looks you in the eye as an equal when you're up there. They look at you as an object. And every object is disposable**. Which is why it annoys me to no end that the world now uses the word "hot" to mean "beautiful." They are NOT the same thing. Neither are "wanted" and "liked." Girls, there's absolutely nothing wrong with wanting to feel "sexy" as long as *your* idea of "sexiness" is grounded in what makes you feel awesome and comfortable and excited inside of your own unique body, whatever shape or size that body might be. It's also normal and natural and OK for you to find other people sexy, too, and to have sexual desire. (It's also completely fine if you really couldn't be any *less* interested in sex, no matter what anyone else says.)

Not long ago, I participated in a global panel of "Top Aspie Mentors" who'd been featured in Dr. Tony Attwood's *Been There. Done That. Try This.* What an honor! Several wonderful Aspie men—dressed in baseball caps, sweaters, sandals, Hawaiian T-shirts, and suits—were on the stage, as were two other bright,

Aspie women. One wore all black and a cowboy hat, the other wore a loose-fitting pants suit. Then there was me, wearing a 1960s-style black-and-white pointelle dress (which I'd bought for a previous event at my church) and my favorite "happy" wardrobe item—red patent leather heels. We spoke for an hour; afterwards, an audience member came up to me and said, "You know what? I saw you walk in here with those red shoes and thought to myself, *Now there's a confident woman!*" I beamed and thanked her (heck, I've fought hard to become that confident chick!). Yet soon afterwards, I learned that another person had taken great umbrage with my shoes, complaining that they were a terrible distraction—an unprofessional attempt to draw attention to my appearance and away from the conversation.

I admit that at first, I was embarrassed. Then hurt. Then flat-out annoyed. Let me ask you: Why did no one comment on the "professionalism" of the men's clothing? Are *red shoes* less professional than a Hawaiian shirt? Or Teva sandals? Or another woman's ten-gallon cowboy hat? No! We were ALL OK being US.

In our various ways, we "Top Mentors" were expressing ourselves as much through our clothing as through the deeply sincere life experiences we shared onstage. Afterwards, the moderator even thanked me for the kindness and humility he felt my words carried to anyone listening…and I know I must've done something right from the achingly beautiful letters I received from mothers, teachers, teens, and twenty-somethings who heard me speak. But you know what? I can't recall a single thing I *did* say that day. Sadly, what I most remember from an occasion that was a personal and professional pinnacle are my shoes, because again I saw that if a woman can't be taken down by attacking the content of her work, the next (but totally irrelevant) target is her sexuality.

Hillary Clinton is an undeniably polarizing, divisive political figure. Still, I've gotta give her this: she's a tough chick. And she hit the nail on the head with this one. "You may not agree with a woman," she said, "but to criticize her appearance—as opposed to her ideas or actions—isn't doing anyone any favors, least of all you. Insulting a woman's looks when they have nothing to do with the issue at hand implies a lack of comprehension on your part, an inability to engage in high-level thinking. You may think whatever you want of her, but everyone else just thinks you're an idiot."

Rejecting or ignoring "traditionally girl" stuff can make people behave terribly. So can being "too successful" at it. But in both cases, the issue isn't you or me. It's THEM.

Girls, *you don't have to attend every argument to which you are invited. At least, you certainly don't have to engage on their terms and participate in your own takedown.* You're running your show. No one else. You. So be the power player. Instead of merely *re*-acting. Think. Choose. ACT.

One month after the panel, I arrived at another conference to discover there was more. Between events, the red shoe gossip had continued as "back channel" phone calls. But it occured to me: phone calls that begin with "I don't want to sound like a mean girl" might as well start off with "I don't want to sound like a racist." It's an instant, undermining disclaimer. If you have to qualify what you say, it's just wrong. And it's sad. So I took a minute to think about what to do. And then I *did* respond.

When we *respond* to a name, a title, a cruel insult, or a loving nickname, we are agreeing that some part of the name fits. That it's appropriate. That somehow, we recognize ourselves in the words we hear—"Too sexy." "Too butch." "Too girlie." "Freakishly neuter." "Prude." "Slut." No, we are none of those things. Whether you put on cargo pants and combat boots or red stilettos is no one else's business, and it certainly has no bearing on the kind of human being you are.

Truth? This whole "how you show your femaleness" game isn't even about sexual roles, morality, or behavior. It's about obedience. About feeling constantly insecure. About jealousy and power. About distracting our energy from everything we *really* have to SAY and DO.

If what you wear—be it a Hawaiian shirt, a ten-gallon hat, or whatever's on the cover of the latest *Vogue*—helps you feel centered and joyful and real, if it helps you find your voice and do good in the world, wear it. Try on a million "costumes." Pick pieces of this and that. Keep what feels right and leave the rest. And the haters? Disagree with them. Or disregard them. You're still figuring yourself out—we all are. You don't owe anyone else comfort. Whomever "you" are today (it may change tomorrow), be her. Write a new character. Shake things up. Change the world. After all, well-behaved women rarely make history.

If you construct your version of "femaleness" based on a world of conflicting directions, it's only natural that you'll feel conflicted. Yes, your sexuality does involve some things you can't control or direct—like your life history, your feelings, other people's reactions; it also includes a whole lot of things that you *can* control. You have the absolute right to say no to anything you are not comfortable with—and to say yes to the things you *are* comfortable with...to assert your desires and your preferences, to educate yourself, and to be safe. So nix the nonsense and try these helpful tips instead:

- How you choose to dress does affect the way a lot of people will interact with you. Not all people, but a lot of them. Work with that. As long as you're making informed choices, you've got power.

- **NOTHING you wear (or don't) gives anyone else the right to touch you without your enthusiastic consent.** I don't care where you are, what you're doing, or who sees you.

- **"Do Not Wear" lists at school/work are fine (sometimes even helpful) IF you get to have a voice in their creation/enforcement AND IF they're based on more than lengths and measurements and degrees of reveal.** Not one single centimeter of you is bad or shameful or dangerous. Not now. Not ever.

- Some clothing choices will serve you better in certain situations than others; however, no part of you or of your clothing is EVER responsible for other people's behavior. Period.

- The neurotypical world interprets a messy/unkempt appearance as unconcerned laziness.

- You need to follow basic grooming practices (you just *do*) to keep healthy and make your body pleasant with which to share space. (This is something I talk more about in *The Asperkid's (Secret) Book of Social Rules*.) It doesn't have to be fussy. You just have to be clean.

- If you want tips on make-up or fashion, my favorite resources are listed in the back of this book. But remember, even those are just options; they are *not* mandates.

The last time I checked, how you dress and how you look has nothing to do with your value as a human or your successful "execution" of "femaleness." However you package yourself, understand yourself, or present yourself, you know what? **There is NO right way—and no wrong way—to be a girl.**

I don't care if you dress in trousers every day
  and never ever put on a lick of make-up.
I don't care if you love high heels
  and vintage perfume bottles.
I don't care if you are attracted to boys,
  girls, both, or nobody in particular.
What we wear isn't what makes us women.
Whom we want to kiss isn't what makes us women.
Tell me this, if you'd tell me what kind of woman you are...
Are you being kind to others? To yourself?
Are you thinking new ideas? Are you exploring?
Are you trying new things?
Are you showing courage and curiosity and generosity?
Good. Because those are the things real women do.
No matter what shoes we wear.

13

The Question Box

Why THAT Would Be a Good Idea (or Not)

Need to Know (and Believe)

- Your body was designed for YOU to understand, control, and enjoy.

- Trusting a search engine to give you the right information is like hitchhiking and expecting to get home safely. Not smart.

- There is nothing bad or shameful or sinful about the very parts which make us female.

- Whatever your particular figure, your body is brilliant and useful.

- Private parts (those covered by bathing suits) should only be discussed and/or touched in private places (rooms with doors) by yourself, a doctor, or an intimate partner.

- No matter your age, religion, culture, or nationality, YOU have complete, inarguable ownership of your body.

- Your body is not a prize to be won, a currency to trade for kindness, or an object to be bought through time, effort, or gifts.

Mr. Sporano was my sixth-grade health teacher, a tricky subject he managed quite well from that third-floor classroom at Grover Cleveland Middle School. It was always artificially warm in there, I remember. Furnaces churning out dry, overly heated air into an oaken room already full of afternoon sunlight. And the subject matter, I'll admit, could make my cheeks grow hot, too. Let's be honest. The word "puberty" is almost as uncomfortable as the subject itself. I am *not* a squeamish, bashful girl, but that is just a seriously awkward word. There's nothing mature or cool-sounding about it. Personally, I hear "puberty" and pretty much think acne, goofy-body-noise humor, and kids bragging about everything they "knew" (which, I can tell you now, was almost absolutely nothing).

However silly, however shy, however all-knowing anyone seemed, Mr. Sporano kept his cool. He was determined to get accurate information through our embarrassed giggles. And we were all secretly glad of it. You see, the playground was fast becoming bra-snapping, dirty-joke central where the worst thing you could be was "babyish." Not mature enough to fill out a bra? You'd be called a "Pirate's Dream" (sunken chest). Throw a temper tantrum or cry "like a baby"? Expect to be beat up for being "a wuss."

That weird territory between kid-dom and adulthood was—and is—well, weird, besides which, it's full of innuendos and lies. Guys swearing to have more "experience" than they do. Girls wondering whether "nice outfit" was meant as a compliment or a subtle dig.

So, yes, every one of us was uncomfortable in Mr. Sporano's classroom. But every one of us also *really* wanted to be there, because Mr. Sporano offered us protection. Health class was defense against social humiliation—you know…the horror of being the only one who doesn't get the lyrics to some new song or makes some accidental locker room gaffe. He was even our respite from the most awful, most embarrassing situation known to tweens or teens anywhere—"The Talk." That hideous moment when an adult, who seems even more embarrassed than you are, tries to stumble awkwardly through some garbled advice that would've sounded pitifully lame even fifty years ago.

The solution to all of our adolescent anxiety was a simple shoebox covered in construction paper and clearly labeled in Mr. Sporano's distinctively perfect print: THE QUESTION BOX. Students could anonymously slip in their secret queries without fear of ridicule. In fact, it was pretty much expected that when Mr. Sporano got around to reading and answering the question aloud in his bold, unwavering voice, whoever actually wrote it would laugh along with everyone else. "Can you even believe somebody asked that?!" we'd all whisper, while secretly, every one of us waited for the answer, an answer we could trust, the truth, thoroughly explained, free of goofiness and without the super-formal textbook terms. Because yeah…we *all* really wanted to know.

Well, here's my first question to you: how are you supposed to know what to do with all of your parts if you don't even know what they're called or what they're for? There have to be at least seventy-three ludicrous names for vagina (including hoo-ha, honeypot, snatch, va-jayjay, and MaryLou), and I cannot even begin to mask my surprise over how many girls think that they urinate out of said "hoo-ha." (You don't.)

Think of this bit as the "Question Box" goes spectrum. Everyone has questions. Everyone. So, while you are getting to know the amazing, unique, precocious you, you absolutely HAVE to include your body in that process.

Truth? We've *all* been there. You know—the feeling that you're supposed to "get" something, but you don't *really* have a clue about whatever it is that everyone else seems to know, so you sort of just smile or laugh, generally nodding along. Ladies, these are *your bodies* we're talking about. Yours. Don't nod along. Don't be embarrassed. Find out what's what, and make it work for you. Like our minds—our bodies are NOT pieces to be judged or owned, tools to sell things, designed just to please others, or weapons to be used against us. From your crown to your soles, you are yours. Period. And no matter what anyone else says or implies, **your body was designed for YOU to understand, control, and enjoy.**

Which brings us to an actual question "Grace" emailed to the "Question Box":

Question: What is "that part" of me supposed to look like?

Answer (part 1): I'm sorry…which part? Your elbow? Your knees? OK, I know what you mean by "that part," but I'm making a point before I answer the question. When you teach a little child the word "nose" or "chin" or "mouth," do you call it "that part"? Of course not. And you don't call any of *those* parts by silly names. Why? because you're not at all embarrassed to say "nose." You don't feel uncomfortable saying "chin." So you don't cover up. You don't avoid it. You just say it.

THERE IS NOTHING MORE RIGHT OR WRONG ABOUT THE WORD "VAGINA" THAN THE WORD "NOSE." **One is more private, yes, and so discussions about and attention to "that part" should take place only with people you know well and trust in rooms with doors— but "private part" does not mean "shameful part."** It means precisely the opposite—something so important as to deserve *more* respect, not less.

When we use word substitutes, what we're saying is that we are not really OK with ourselves, that there's something bad or shameful or sinful about the very parts which make us female. Basically, we're being sexist. And remember, we teach the world how to treat us. How can we expect better from anyone else than we are willing to give ourselves? **That said, if you know the right words and are comfortable saying them, it's perfectly OK to have a sense of humor sometimes, too.**

Answer (part 2): What does a "typical" woman look like? There are some basics, sure. Two arms. Two legs. Breasts. But what about height? Weight? Skin color? Hair length? There are no "normals"—no "right" or "better" except what a society artificially *decides* to celebrate. Otherwise, there's no inherent positive or negative in however you happen to be built. Your hands and mine may not be the same size. My eyes may be lighter than yours. That kind of variation doesn't come as a big surprise, right? Well, just extend the idea a little further. The shape of our eyes may vary—and both are completely fine. So can the shape of our breasts and bottoms. And it's ALL GOOD. Because, girls, there's no "supposed to" when it comes to how your body looks—even "down there."

A Whole New Level of Personal Space Issues

In *The Asperkid's (Secret) Book of Social Rules*, I talk about how mixed-up personal boundaries can feel for those of us on the spectrum and how we can avoid "popping others' comfort bubbles"—personal spaces that include ideas, things, conversations, and even relationships.

This book, however, is about girl issues, so instead of "outer space," the area around our bodies, I want to point out the importance of "inner space." For women, **our sexuality involves allowing another person entry way past just being within our personal space—it involves entry within our person.**

No matter your age, religion, culture, or nationality, YOU have complete, inarguable ownership of your body. Period. And, as sole owner of your body, ONLY YOU can choose how you express yourself, have agency over pleasure, determine how you relate to others, and who you want to let inside. This isn't small stuff.

Trusting a Search Engine Is Like Hitchhiking

You've probably heard that one of our "special spectrum quirks" is the literal way we interpret language. Like how, a month after she'd had spinal neurosurgery, I told my four-year-old daughter to hop into the shower. So she did. Hop, that is. And then she slipped on the wet floor and fell. Hard. (Soooo not good.)

Sometime during the past year, I learned that English-speaking Europeans call the punctuation mark at the end of a sentence a "full stop." That is a very, very good idea. In the US, we call it a "period." And yes, my European sisters, we *also* call your "time of the month" a "period." Which leaves a big, fat space for serious misunderstanding. Well, I may have managed the most cringe-worthy gaff of all, my friends. And now, I'm about to reveal it in print, for everyone to see, for all time. (That's how much I love y'all!)

When I first started hearing about "getting your period," there were a lot of other words being thrown in the mix of those confusing conversations...egg, ovulate, menstruate (and was it pronounced "stroo" or not?). Well, I guess I sort of clung to the few that were familiar to me: egg and period. A period was a little round dot. An egg was also round...well, roundish. As far as I was getting this, when you "got your period," you had released an egg. Like the ones you'd buy at the grocer's, it remained unfertilized, and (yep, I was still thinking chicken-ish), your body got rid of it. Curious and not quite sure about what I was supposed to be expecting for myself, I asked my mom if, the next time she got her period, I could see it. (Oh, if I could suck those words back in...) Basically, she shot me an utterly pinched, horrified look, shouted, "NO! OF COURSE NOT!" and walked out of the room. Obvious mistake, Jenny. Only, I had no idea whatsoever what my mistake had been…

- Throw in some years of experience, and I've figured this much out—worthwhile information if you've been menstruating for years or if you're still waiting for the arrival of "Aunt Flo": If you haven't yet gotten your period and want to know what it might look like when you do start, try putting a few drops of red food coloring in the crotch panel of an old pair of panties. That's what you'll see…because human women do not, in fact, lay eggs. (Ugh.)

- You should never, ever be made to feel that a genuine question is dumb or that you are gross for asking it. If you ask an honest question and get a shaming response, ask someone else. The problem wasn't the question—it was the answer.

- Spectrum folks learn by intellectualizing, right? That means when we want to understand something, WE DO RESEARCH. In general, that's good. **BUT when it comes to sex and your body, DO NOT JUST GO FACT HUNTING, PLEASE!** When we investigate on our own, we often find very disturbing, very inaccurate, or very misleading information that can scar self-image, create awful misrepresentations of *good* things, and even damage relationships permanently—only we won't know we've gotten the wrong information until after the damage is done.

- Sex as you see it online, in movies, in books—*that* version of sex is false. DO NOT use it to learn what other people will find attractive, to show what *real* women like, how we act, look, or what relationships usually include. It's fiction, pure and simple. Sex, on the other hand, and the consequences of sex, are very, very real.

- Imagination and wild ideas are wonderful for art and literature, but when those ideas affect your body and your lifestyle, this is bad stuff. When your fantasy ideal of the human body doesn't even exist in nature, and definitely not in your average person, how are you going to feel when your body doesn't look like that? Simple answer: not good enough. EVER.

- **Trusting a search engine to give you the right information is like hitchhiking and expecting to get home safely.** Not smart. **IF YOU WANT MORE INFORMATION, USE THE RESOURCES AT THE BACK OF THIS BOOK.** You can trust them to be honest, up-front, and ACCURATE.

- Real sources of information are going to give you concrete information that can help you think about your own sex life, and reliable information that could even save your life.

Why Would THAT Be a Good Idea?

And now we arrive at a very, very important question about sex that I've been asked by multiple young women: *Why would I want to do that* (sexual intercourse)? *It sounds awful and painful!* **The first part of my answer is simple: there is NOTHING that you should want. Nothing. Allowing or going along with something because someone else wants to or "convinces" you to is not the same as desiring it yourself.** To be physically intimate with you, a partner needs to be able to say much more than "she didn't say 'no.'" He or she must know that whatever you do, you're doing with certainty and enthusiasm.

    The second part of my answer is that the question itself is wrong. Spectrum minds tend to jump to all-or-nothing responses. But "sex" isn't all or nothing. Putting anyone's individual values and morals aside, you don't start off one day without having ever held hands with anyone and decide you want to "go all the way" that night. There are lots and lots (and LOTS) of emotional and physical experiences that need to happen before intercourse— before you'd even WANT intercourse. It'd be a bit like expecting to want to do a calculus problem without having tried counting first. That's not only full steam ahead, it's full steam over a cliff, headed for a crash-and-burn.

Sensory-wise, emotionally, physically, and intellectually, you *wouldn't* want anything inside you without your mind and body being given time to get used to (let alone interested in) the idea. That's why rape is so physically painful. **If your mind doesn't actively want something to happen, your body won't either.** You won't produce any natural lubrication, your muscles will be tense, and delicate tissues can be seriously hurt. That's *not* what sex is supposed to be—in fact, it's pretty much darned the opposite.

Remember that "sexuality" includes "sensuality," which means only choosing activities that your body wants and likes. Remember, too, that sexuality includes "emotional closeness." Allowing someone to enter you (physically) requires that you trust them to like you for exactly who you are, with all of your quirks and imperfections. That they be aware of your wonderfulness, too. It requires the investment of time and maturity—learning to be comfortable with your own body and with your partner's, paying attention to what *both* people like or dislike and responding accordingly. It means asking for what you enjoy and feeling safe to say no to whatever you don't enjoy, without fear of abandonment or punishment. Letting someone enter your body requires that you both know and believe that this person will not hurt you. It means being aware of all of the *very real* consequences that sex can have and knowing that you have *both* planned for them. It means that you are allowing someone to literally be taken inside of you and, for that time, be a part of your physical form. This might sound a little hokey, but it really can be a profound moment of connection.

Eight Tidbits Real Women Wish Someone Had Told Them

1. Your partner isn't a mind reader. You have to communicate (I like this, I don't like this, I have no idea what I'm doing!).

2. Sex doesn't actually look like it does in movies, magazines, or TV. It's messy. It can be goofy and awkward. It can have consequences. Zippers stick. People use protection.

3. You are not more valuable as a person if someone wants to have sex with you, and you are not less valuable as a person if you choose not to have sex.

4. Sex and love are not the same thing. At all.

5. Anxieties and fears about sex are totally normal, and it's (more than) fine to talk about them.

6. Your body is not a prize to be won, a currency to trade for kindness, or an object to be bought through time, effort, or gifts.

7. There's nothing you should or shouldn't want. There's no expiration date and no due-by date, either. This isn't a race.

8. Your life is yours. Your body is yours. What you do or don't do is no one's business but yours.

Take the time to get to know yourself—*all* of yourself. And then, tell the world to keep its superficial, flippant judgments to itself. Other people's perceptions of you are reflections of *their own* concerns, not of your value. And if you don't believe me, then take it from the altogether fantabulous Miss Piggy (because really, who's gonna argue with *her?!*): "Beauty is in the eye of the beholder, and, from time to time, it may be necessary to give a misinformed beholder a black eye."

14

Body Blow

How You "Measure Up"

THERE ARE 4 SHAPES...

1.) APPLE

2.) PEAR

3.) HOURGLASS

AND...

YOU

4.) AWESOME

Need to Know (and Believe)

- Most things that sound as if they're about looks or body image really aren't—they're about feeling wanted, approved of, worthwhile. Or about not feeling any of those things.

- A well-meant compliment deserves gracious acceptance.

- How you handle compliments gives a public glimpse of your self-worth and clear instructions on how the world should treat you.

- Learn the "Five Steps to Compliment Comfort"—an easy system to help consider both the strengths others notice and any constructive feedback they offer, too.

Not too long ago, another spectrum gal and I were talking about bullying. Well, mostly, she was talking, and I'd been listening. After a little while, I nodded. Yep. This was stuff I really understood. I'd been there, too. The truth is, I don't really remember any other specifics of our talk, because all that stuck with me was her next comment. "I don't get it," she said, shaking her head at me. "You're way too pretty to be bullied."

Huh?? OK, that might be one of the most ridiculous things I've ever heard. Ever. Being "pretty" or "sexy" does NOT make you immune from hurt, bullying, or loneliness. Insecurity plagues us all.

If I wanted, I could get all intellectual about body image right now. About girls "hating on" other girls. About beauty myths. I could talk about how every culture has different ideas of what it means to be physically attractive…how one hundred years ago, clothing sizes didn't even exist—so you wouldn't ever find yourself freaking out in a public place about whether you were "small," "medium," or "large." Heck, you wouldn't freak out about it in private, either. There was no such thing as a "size twelve," let alone a size double zero (which means *what* exactly? that you count for less than nothing?). Then again, there most certainly *were* ideas of what it meant to be beautiful—and yes, women and girls knew that whatever kind of lives they hoped to live would probably be tied up, somehow, in how they looked. Whether in ancient Rome, medieval London, the year your mother graduated from high school, or last week in your neighborhood, whatever qualities a given time and place calls "beautiful" have everything to do with power, money, and influence—and a whole lot less to do with flawless skin or a tiny waist.

I *could* get all intellectual about the whole "lookism" thing (and I really want to), but I won't, because then we'd be missing the bigger picture. **Most things that sound as if they're about looks or body image really aren't. Instead, they're about feeling wanted, approved of, worthwhile. Or about not feeling any of those things. About the longing and loneliness if you're not included. About the fear that you'll lose it all if you are. About trying to create some sense of control or reliable logic amidst all the mess and chaos.**

Now I'm going to throw you a complete change-up. I'm going to tell you how I began my reply to my friend. I said, "Thank you." And here's why: The idea that someone can avoid being bullied because of good looks is totally ludicrous. But buried somewhere underneath a miasma of you've-got-to-be-kidding-me ridiculousness, there was a sincerely intended kindness. **And a well-meant compliment deserves gracious acceptance. That's a basic social skill. More importantly, how you handle compliments gives a public glimpse of your self-worth and clear instructions on how the world should treat you.**

Most of us, without realizing it, seek out relationships and situations that match the way we already see ourselves, even if that means reinforcing our insecurities by choosing "mean girl" friends or insulting dating partners. If you believe you're unattractive, hearing even the most sincere compliment about your appearance is scary—it feels like a trick. If you believe you're not very smart and someone honestly praises your thinking, you're apt to feel that you're being teased. If you believe you're very hard to love, you may just figure that no matter how hard you try, everyone will end up hating you. Believing someone's kind words, then, only feels like a giant setup for heartbreak.

For many spectrum girls, rejecting compliments and believing insults is just more comfortable—we're not sure whom to trust, and we probably hear a lot more of the rough stuff. You could say the volume on the negative dial is louder as a result. And more than that, **accepting even honest compliments means confronting how very little we actually believe in ourselves. So we skip that part. We dismiss appreciation or admiration (unintentionally insult the other person's opinion) and smother it all under a nice, thick layer of self-deprecation.**

Well-meaning adults will (or at least, really should) tell you to love yourself, to accept yourself—to be bold, "lean in," and ask for what you want. But another social pitfall awaits—unspoken afterthoughts that we simply don't hear: Do your best (but don't show anyone up). Love yourself (but not too much). Be confident (but not too loudly). Be yourself (just not like that).

Girls, this whole compliment business is a field full of social landmines. One "mind-blind" misstep, and very genuine modesty is read as false…hard-won confidence is renamed "arrogance." And there we go…sliding back into the land of I-can't-do-anything-right-anyway. So it seems to me that we need **a trustworthy, balanced strategy to help us filter the confusion and noise, an easy system to help consider both the strengths others notice and any constructive feedback they offer, too.**

And now, we have it—five steps to compliment comfort:

1. **Look her in the "third eye."** Eye contact tells the speaker that you are paying attention and listening respectfully. However, it can also be a serious distraction to a lot of us. So focus on the spot on the bridge of the other person's nose, right between her eyes (a spot called the third eye in Hinduism and certain other Eastern spiritual traditions). She'll feel heard, and you'll be able to stay engaged.

2. **Nod.** This does NOT mean you agree. It's just a nonverbal sign that you are listening.

3. **Stay silent or say "hmm" in consideration.** Allowing the other person to finish speaking is just polite; nothing more, nothing less.

4. **Thank the person for telling you what she thinks.** Whether you agree or disagree isn't the issue. You're showing appreciation for communication, which is always a good thing.

5. **Decide**—later, on your own. Think about everything privately (and refer to *The Asperkid's (Secret) Book of Social Rules* for how to determine whether or not to believe what you hear).

Actual Hunger

Remember I told you that body image has nothing to do with food or weight, and everything to do with feeling accepted? Well, let's face it, sisters: Being left out is what many of us have come to expect. We aren't just *hungry* to be wanted—we're starving. And though we'd never say as much out loud (being the strong, sassy chicks we are), it's not a far stretch to say that broken hearts will *do* anything—*believe* anything—to matter.

There is no one on earth who can give you self-esteem. No one who can tie a bow around confidence and offer it to you. I sure would if I could. But self-esteem is the one and only thing that absolutely MUST come from you.

OK, I'll admit that I heard that idea a lot growing up. But in truth, I thought it was *wrong*. Compliments—when I came by them—certainly *did* make me feel better about myself. A self-esteem boost for sure, thank you very much. But it turned out there was a flaw in the plan, after all.

Self-esteem cannot come from what you are or what you have. "You are *so* pretty...you are *so* smart...you have the *best* hair" aren't accomplishments. They're comparisons—debatable opinions—judgments made by other people about things we can't even control. (And not for nothing, girls, but no one evaluated Steve Jobs based on his bottom.) Think about it: We're measured by the way we curve (or don't), by where we're flat (or not) or round or sharp. We're reduced to dimensions and inches and the pull of gravity on our bodies when we step on a scale. Yet inside, we are unquantifiable. Gigglefests and dreams, ambition and generosity.

Your body does not come with a lifetime warranty, but it does come with a lifetime guarantee. Nurture it, fuel it, cherish it.

~Karen Krejcha

Remember, in every competition, there is both a winner *and* loser. And in turns and cycles, we will each be both, again and again, without guarantees. So, please don't surrender your self-worth to someone else's assessment. **Let's measure ourselves by the things we can control, by who we are now and who we are working (very hard) to become...through purposeful**

action. Let's value the behaviors we choose, the effort we put in, and—most of all—the courage we summon when we feel afraid and we do it anyway. If we survive on "you are so…" compliments, we will be slain by "you are so…" criticism. Please, let's be easier on ourselves. Let's be gentle. And fair. And far too beautiful to be measured.

15

Function Over Form

Your Shape, Senses...and Bras

Need to Know (and Believe)

- When we don't see ourselves reflected back (truthfully) anywhere in what's supposed to be "our culture" (mainstream or spectrum), we are reduced everywhere.

- A scale just shows your numerical relationship to gravity! It doesn't measure talent, beauty, possibility, strength, or love.

- Your body wasn't created to be observed. It exists to do.

- Lingerie (bras and panties) should feel comfortable and beautiful to you, protect your modesty, and allow you to move as you'd like. Your underwear has nothing to do with pleasing anyone else.

My friend, Amanda, has really lovely skin. Betsy's hair is naturally bouncy and thick. And Brigid's smile is simply joyous. Funny, isn't it, how we can see the beauty in our best friends, sisters, mothers, and aunts without the slightest thought to their flaws… but can obsess for hours on our own "imperfections?" We fixate to the point where we avoid summertime fun at the beach or hide when someone takes a picture. It seems to me that in a million little ways, girls are constantly trying to disappear—to hide in plain sight—to avoid any actual record that "I was here!" In our warped minds, photos become Facebook-plastered, frozen-in-time mirrors. Instead of happy memories, they're dissectible canvases that we can stare at as we pick apart our features over and over again.

Invisibility is about feeling disconnected—from the people around us and even from ourselves. And for women on the autism spectrum, that's particularly true. We don't see ourselves actively or accurately reflected almost anywhere. **Whether it's TV, movies, or novels, odds are that even an "Aspie-type" female character won't be labeled. She's just the quirky one. Or the brainiac. Or the freak. She's not a real person; she's a stereotype. A blanket "other" whose "character" explains away any need to understand her or love her or even see her. Us.**

When we don't see ourselves reflected back (truthfully) anywhere in what's supposed to be "our culture" (mainstream or spectrum), we are reduced everywhere. We are insignificant. Unreal. Invisible. That, I'm quite sure, is why people are always surprised when they learn I have Asperger's. They have no reality-based idea of how a woman on the spectrum might *actually* look, sound, or think. And without some concept to use as a standard, they can't "recognize" me—or you. We're not quite like "them," and we're left out of the spectrum, too. That's a serious disconnect. Serious shame. And blame. And invisibility. And it makes us very easy, very acceptable targets.

So, I have a suggestion: Let's stop agreeing to vanish. Let's refuse to fade away. Let's be present for this life. Let's live out loud and, in the time we've got, let the world know we're alive. As the saying goes, "Well-behaved women rarely make history." Let's try this instead:

~~Petite~~ *Smart*

~~Tiny~~ *Kind*

~~Small~~ *Brave*

~~Delicate~~ *Creative*

~~Thin~~ *Funny*

~~Skinny~~ *Talented*

~~Dainty~~ *Strong*

~~Fragile~~ *Fearless*

Bits and Pieces

Today, I was talking about body shapes with a young woman I know. "Well," she asked, "what about me? My face, for example. Is it a good shape or a bad one?" My answer: "Yes." She looked confuzzled. "What? That doesn't make sense," she argued. "Oh yes it does," I replied. "There's no such thing as 'good' or 'bad' when it comes to face shape, or body shape, or hair texture, or food. It is what it is. A donut isn't inherently 'bad.' It's dough, for Pete's sake. A square-shaped face isn't inherently 'good' or 'bad' either. It's a head. It has a shape. That's it. Sometimes, a description is just a description—it's not a judgment. It just is."

Girls, we have to stop thinking of ourselves as carved up parts to evaluate. Easier said than done, though, I know. Most of the time, when we watch television or movies, when we see ads online or in magazines, male bodies are presented as either a close-up face (as if we were having a conversation) or as a whole-body shot. They're active. Walking. Running. Jumping. Building. Dodging. Women, on the other hand, are more often shown in parts and pieces. A close-up of a bum. Or breasts. Or a torso. The result is that our entire society is accustomed to thinking of men as entire people. Women and girls, however, are thought of more as *parts* of people. Guys don't sit around analyzing their nail beds, bikini lines, earlobes, eyebrow symmetry, cellulite, or any one of the countless "bits" girls do. For goodness' sake, a scale just shows your numerical relationship to gravity! It doesn't measure talent, beauty, possibility, strength, or love.

If we allow our perseveration-prone parts-loving minds to believe—for one minute—that just a little bit more exercise will make the day better, that one size smaller is really all you need, that you simply *cannot* go to the beach with your family looking like *this*, that perfection (and all the smiles and friends and dates and self-esteem that go along with it) is just one more salad away…we will have completely lost touch with what our bodies are meant for in the first place.

A body is not a bunch of parts to dissect and judge. A body is a symphony. A single organism. A well-coordinated whole that *does*. It sings. It dances. It gives birth. It dies. It laughs. It carries. It saunters and tiptoes. It shoves and punches. It rests. It grows. It wiggles and squirms and coughs. It digests. It breathes. It listens and watches and tastes and touches. It caresses. It lingers. It waits. It hugs. It yawns and stretches and swims and types. It pees. It burps. It snuggles. It lives.

Your body wasn't created to be observed. It exists to do. Look, in this world, form follows function (something's shape is determined by its job). Try cutting a steak with a spoon. Not too effective. Try eating ice cream with a steak knife. Not too safe. The design of a thing has everything to do with its task. The same is true for your body. You have five toes on each foot because that's the ideal weight distribution to keep your balance. You have eyes that shut automatically whenever you sneeze to prevent germs from flying into them. Your body looks like it does only because of the actions it needs to accomplish. **So go throw like a girl. Run like a girl. Slam dunk it in their faces like a girl.**

You know what else? Life doesn't wait until you "get thin" enough (which is what, exactly?) to deserve to be living it. Life is happening *right now*. And for heaven's sake, you're entitled to be part of it. Quite frankly, sisters, your bodies can do amazing things. And they deserve a whole lot more respect than they've been given.

When I was admitted to the hospital for anorexia, I was 106 pounds (48 kilograms). At 5 feet 8 inches (1.7 meters) tall, that put me at a dangerously low body-fat percentage with a checklist of consequences (besides the steadily declining numbers that still felt like victory to me). I'd stopped getting my period (because my body wouldn't be able to sustain a pregnancy), was cold all the time, dreamt about food every night (a physical marker of starvation), and had begun to have random fainting spells—once, while driving! It all seems surreal to me now, but you can't really argue with the facts. Things were pretty serious.

I was an inpatient for a month—and goodness, how I wish the doctor had known about Asperger's in women back then.

He didn't, though. So they *guessed* at how to help me. Guessed at what might be underlying the behavior that was endangering my life. And for the most part, they didn't guess very well.

There was one smart activity, though, that I remember even now, years later. At the time the psychologist suggested it, I will be very honest—this plan sounded like the most ridiculous bunch of feel-good gobbledygook I'd heard to that point. You know what? I was wrong. It may have been the only really insightful tool I took away from the experience. I can't remember the name, so for now, we'll just call it "An Apology and Thank You to My Legs." Give it a read—and then think about what a letter to *your* body might say.

Dear Legs,

I'm sorry for all the times I've pinched you or measured you with my hands. I'm sorry for the times I've hated you or slapped you or made you keep running or cycling or climbing even when you were too tired and sore and deserved a rest. I'm sorry for deciding whether you were good enough by which size jeans fit right now. I'm sorry I called you names. None of those things were very nice, especially because you never stopped being nice to me. So, thank you for walking me around my yard to trim daddy's rosebushes. I'll bet he's smiling down on them. Thank you for pushing the gas pedal when I wanted to go to the store. I get to be independent because of you. Thank you for kicking off the blankets and helping me sleep better. Thank you for getting me up the stairs (quickly!) when I forgot my wallet and it was time to go. Thank you for helping me to climb the trees and push the tire swing. Thank you for dancing in the kitchen with my dog. Thank you for doing some seriously rockin' kick boxing and an absolutely wicked triple-time step in perfect time. I guess what I'm saying is...thank you for being completely awesome.

I hereby promise to...

* be grateful for you exactly the way you are

* love and appreciate you for what you DO

* offer you the healthy foods and drinks you need, plus the playtime, laughter, silliness, and exercise that help you feel good

* clothe you in things that feel good

* listen to the messages you send me and accept that you deserve to be healthy

* honor you as a unique creation that's bigger and brighter than anyone's opinion, capable of more things than I've discovered.

It's amazing to get to live with you. So, thank you. You're perfect.

Love, The Me Inside

Girl-Fabulous Sensory-Friendly Body Stuff: Q&A

Bras Meet Sensory Savvy

Q: My mom says it's time for me to start wearing a bra. The trouble is that everything she buys is way too uncomfortable to wear. I've tried on sports bras, but they're too tight. I've tried loads of regular bras, too, and I can't handle the buckle and hooks—they drive me so crazy that I can't even think straight! My mom's being really nice, only she says she doesn't have any more ideas. Do you?

A: Yeah, real bras aren't quite as practical as all those under-dressed, under-supported superheroes would have you believe, are they? (I mean, really—can you imagine the wind resistance of trying to fly with exposed cleavage?!)

So, if you're going to be super in any capacity, let's tackle this one. First, the question I usually hear is, "Why do I have to wear a bra?"

Well, you don't *have* to wear one; however, there are some physical realities of which to be aware. Your nipples are made of a special kind of tissue that contracts when you get cold or when something rubs up against them (it's your body's clue that a baby wants to nurse and needs a latch). A bra places a layer of nonmoving material between your nipple and your shirt. Reduced friction means your nipples won't contract and poke out as much, and the extra cloth means that even if they do "wake up," your body isn't on display to everyone. Without the bra, others can, essentially, see parts of you that aren't meant for public display.

Next, lingerie, worn correctly, is about choosing pieces that feel comfortable to you, allow you to move as you'd like, and that *you* think are beautiful. A lot of people have the wackadoodle idea that undergarments are for someone *else's* appreciation. They're not! Just like your sexuality as a whole, when you are comfortable in your own skin, when you get to a place of being able to say, "Yes, I want this, but no, I don't like that," you will exude the confidence that will make *any* lingerie you wear seem appealing…because it will be on a young woman who completely owns who she is and what she does.

Now, then—getting used to wearing a bra is always kind of a mind-and-body experience. It's a marker of real change, and that can bring up a lot of real feelings—some good, maybe some confused. Be sure you talk with someone you trust, if you need. You won't be the first to feel ANYTHING, I promise. That also goes for other girls: If you WISH your mom would buy you a bra, even if you don't "need" one. If other girls are wearing them and no one at your house has offered to get you one, it's OK to ask. Just explain that it will make you feel "more comfortable."

But if your mom is onboard (like yours is!) and the problem is sensory, then I've got a couple of ideas for you to try:

- This may sound strange—but really, who cares? What you want to get is called a "leisure" or "sleeping bra," although you can absolutely wear them when you are wide awake. Basically, the fit is soft cotton, the support is gentle (not squashy), and there are NO HOOKS OR BUCKLES involved. The "sounds strange" part is that these bras are usually sold to women who have JUST had babies. Often, new mothers want extra-comfy support because their bodies feel super-sensitive—which is how Aspies' bodies may ALWAYS feel! So, the need (and solution) is pretty darn similar.

- There are also some "sensory friendly" bra companies that make pieces worth trying. (Check the back of the book for resources.)

16

Why *Romeo and Juliet* Is Not a Love Story

Need to Know (and Believe)

- When you love someone, the idea of living without him or her may be heartbreaking and sad, but it does not mean the world is over.

- The all-or-nothing, now-or-never, this-person-or-all-is-lost feelings of *Romeo and Juliet* is what we're taught to expect out of love and romance.

- "Violence" isn't about hitting any more than eating disorders are about food. It's about taking away your control over your own mind, heart, and body.

- Self-advocacy is teaching other people to treat us with dignity and respect. It is asking for what we deserve, and not accepting anything less.

I am probably about to make Shakespeare purists furious the world over…but here we go anyway: *Romeo and Juliet* is NOT a love story. It's not. There's no love in it. It's a tragedy about the dangers of infatuation and acting impulsively without stopping to get all of the information first. You could almost say it's a lesson on how *not* to do a love story. (And I guess I just did say it—so there!)

Alright, in case it's been a while since you visited the Montagues and Capulets, let me refresh your memory. The whole thing starts with a young man who is nearly suicidal because the "love of his life" is not interested in him.

(**Clue #1: When you love someone, the idea of living without him or her may be heartbreaking and sad, but it does not mean the world is over.** That kind of thinking, friends, is called dependence. It's *not* healthy in your own head. And if a partner threatens self-harm, that is a serious indication of control issues.)

But back to poor Romeo. Woe-is-he. Mr. M. got shot down by his crush (Rosalyn), and now he can't imagine how he'll go on. We've all been there. But that's wounded pride. Rejection.

Disappointment. Not love. Alrighty, though, the boys are gonna cheer up their bud. C'mon, Romeo, it's off to a party—and hey! Looks like he's moved on quickly. Just one dance and he's already hooked up with a new chick. (That whole undying devotion for Rosalyn is lookin' pretty thin now!)

Things go back to Mopeyville pretty fast, though. Dang it, but the new girl's turned out to be daddy's enemy's daughter. No worries, though. She's cool with him being a bad boy from the wrong side of the tracks. So—and here's **Clue #2 that this is not a love story**—**they decide to get married. In secret. After having known each other for...maybe eight hours? Power plays. Teenage rebellion. Father issues. Not love.**

Still having known each other for less than twenty-four hours, Romeo and Juliet tie the knot. However, actual relationships not, apparently, being his strong point, the groom kills his new wife's cousin shortly after the wedding. Dang. Now Romeo's got to get out of town before he's arrested.

Which leads us to **Clue #3**! **Does he take his new bride with him? Nope, he just worries about his own skin**. To be fair, Juliet doesn't really seem to want to leave anyway—which maybe makes sense as she's known her now-dead cousin for her entire life and known her hubby for about a day. Ahh, the clear signs of true love: protect yourself and generally bail when the going gets tough (that's me being sarcastic, gals).

When the newlyweds do start thinking about how, maybe, they could smooth out this whole mess, they don't even consider—oh, I don't know—honesty...responsibility...dealing with the consequences of their actions like grown-ups. Nope! Let's just create drama! That's always a smart and emotionally healthy way to fix things. More drama. Oh yes—and an utter lack of communication.

We begin with Juliet faking her own death. Not having actually made certain that she and Romeo were "using their words" and actively listening, too, there's a snafu. Romeo hears the rumor that she's dead, finds her (not actually dead) body, and kills himself. Hello, rash impulsivity. Would Juliet want you to kill yourself, R? No. Not an emotionally stable move. And of course, when Juliet wakes to find her husband's corpse, she kills herself for realsies.

OK, folks, you've got to know: This isn't romance. It's hormones, bad communication, and incredibly impulsive, short-sighted infatuation.

To many of us intense-experience-seeking, emotionally vulnerable spectrum gals, super-high highs and heartbreakingly low lows are how we've come to envision true love. And trust me. You'll be able to find lots of partners out there who'll live up to those ideas. **Those relationships can feel magnetic at first. Irresistible. But they're not. Heck, they aren't even about love. They're about control. And they're very, very dangerous.**

The Good Stuff

Healthy romantic relationships, like all *real* friendships, evolve— they don't happen overnight (no matter how badly we wish they would). In *The Asperkid's (Secret) Book of Social Rules*, one of the most important things I talk about is the idea that, although we often don't see them clearly, the world actually contains many levels of friendship. Picture a pyramid with five levels of closeness; people HAVE to pass THROUGH the "most people you know" bottom rungs to get to the few, trusted, intimate top spots. Think of it as letting them earn their way up. Go slowly. Only time really tells who is a friend, a confidante, a dating partner…and who isn't.

When we give our hearts away too quickly (which is easy to do if you're lonely or not used to being the center of anyone's attention), we forget to value ourselves and things get *bad*. We may get desperate or clingy, or come on too fast or too strong. We may share information that neurotypicals think is too personal way too fast and hold onto friends too jealously. In the end, this kind of behavior makes neurotypicals feel as if they've been hit by a tidal wave. They run. Or they take advantage of us. Think about it: Cinderella didn't need to take off her dress to get her Prince Charming. And neither do you.

Having just ANY person in your life is NOT better than having NO one.

Teaching the World How to Treat You

Self-advocacy is teaching other people to treat us with dignity and respect. It is asking for what we deserve, and not accepting anything less. If you tolerate poor treatment, you teach people to treat you poorly. If you politely and calmly demand what your deserve, you teach them that you expect respect, fairness, and honesty. Do you cooperate—maybe without realizing it—with people who hurt you, or tease you, or leave you out? If you buy into the junk bullies say, if you look in the mirror and feed the lies back to yourself, then yes, you do. **You are helping those who misunderstand or mistreat you. You're bullying yourself, and there is no dignity in that. To bother or not to bother. That is the question.**

Big, fat truth time: The world is full of awesome, creative, kind people. The world is also full of unhappy people with lots of their own insecurities and misconceptions. These folks tend to act like poopeyheads. Grumpy, critical, ick-meisters. And they're everywhere.

So the question is, when said poopeyheads mess with you, how do you decide whether or not to spend the energy on engaging with them? Staying focused is hard enough for a lot of us. How do you know if this is worth the emotional energy it's going to take away from everything else you have going on? Simple. Ask yourself this question:

Is this person (and his or her ickiness) standing between me and something I want (to have, to be, or to do)?

If the answer is no, don't waste your time. Maybe she's a serious annoyance or he's a daily hassle. Not pleasant, I know. But your energy—your attention, your time, your talent—is better spent doing an amazing job at whatever it is you care about most. Concentrate on your work. Surpass expectations. And someday, when you are out there changing the world because of the hard work you're putting in now, you won't be thinking about them at all. Seriously. That really *is* the way it works.

If the answer is yes, then it's gonna be time to step up.
Think of water. It's not exactly potent stuff—but when its energy
is concentrated, it will flow around, under, and over anything
in its way. Just look at the Grand Canyon. There's your proof.
Water—persistent, dodgy water—carved that entire gaping hole
in the crust of the earth. And I'm pretty sure that you are smarter
than a river. All you have to do is think, *Instead of bashing my head
against the rock that is a poopeyhead, how can I be like water—and get
around him?*

"Haters" are gonna hate. And that has nothing to do
with you. You, my friends, are not the designated "Hater
Whisperer." So focus on being what you are and doing
your stuff. And in the meanwhile, remind the world what
you deserve.

Self-advocacy happens in a series of steps:

1. **Know Your Strengths, Know Your Needs**
   We spectrum girls have some strengths in common. For
   example, as a group we have great:

   • passion for our interests

   • compassion

   • honesty

   • integrity

   • loyalty

   • logical and analytical thinking

   • mechanical abilities

   • creative abilities.

We also have some characteristics that present specific needs:

We have these characteristics...	So we often have these needs...
Intense focus on a special interest.	Reminders to ask about others' interests and not do all the talking.
Sincerity, trustworthiness, and loyalness.	Group of trusted neurotypicals who will help us see others' (less honest) motivations.
Impulsiveness.	Strategies to calm ourselves and help us wait before acting or speaking.
All-or-nothing thinking.	Problem-solving techniques, help including others' ideas.
Anxiety.	Coping techniques (like exercise, role-playing social situations, or just knowing who/how to ask for help).

2. **Identify Your Goals**

You are the main character in your own life story. You are the only one who can set the goals and make them happen. If you want something badly enough, you will find a way; if not, you will find an excuse. While you might think that your goal is to punch a bully in the face or to somehow get revenge on the mean girls, that's not true. Well, not *really*.

Every day in every situation, you will feel better if you:

- stay true to your values

- say what you mean and mean what you say

- learn something new

- are brave and move forward, even when you are afraid

- remember that you cannot be conquered unless you allow it.

So don't allow it. Stay focused. What do you *really* want out of this moment? **Choose one or two SPECIFIC, MEASURABLE GOALS that are within your control.** For example: I want to ask that person to have coffee with me. (The goal is *asking*, not getting a "yes." You can't control that.) Ask for advice. Choose someone you really admire to be a mentor who will help you make your goals crystal-clear. Then, stay calm. And keep breathing.

3. **Know Your Rights, Accept Your Responsibilities**
   Your rights and responsibilities change from situation to situation. **Everywhere**, you have the right to expect that other people will:

   • be honest with you

   • keep their promises

   • speak politely to you

   • touch you in kind ways, and only if you say it is OK

   • apologize when they have done wrong

   • speak only truth about you

   • stand up for you ("don't tell me what they said about me, tell me why they felt comfortable saying it to *you*" is how to challenge a "friend" who doesn't have your back).

   However, you should also expect that they **won't** always do as they should. That's when it's up to you to communicate—to teach them how to treat you.

4. **Communicate with Others**
   Explain your ideas using three-part "I" statements:

   a. **"I feel or felt (adjective) when you...(describe the behavior)."**

   b. **What is the effect on you? Tell how the behavior affects you specifically.**

   c. **"I'd prefer or like...(what you want)."**

   An example would be: "I felt disappointed when you didn't call like you said you would. I was looking forward to talking, and honestly, could've done something else if I'd known you were busy. I'd like you to please understand that I won't wait around again if you don't call a second time."

And once you find yourself in some kind of "closer" friendship, remember:

- **Compromise.** Disagreements are a natural part of healthy relationships, but it's important that you find a way to compromise if you disagree on something. Try to solve conflicts in a fair and rational way.

- **Be supportive.** Offer reassurance and encouragement to your partner. Also, let your partner know when you need their support. Healthy relationships are about building each other up, not putting each other down.

- **Respect each other's privacy.** Just because you're in a relationship, that doesn't mean you have to share everything and constantly be together. A little bit of distance is a GOOD thing—even when you're madly in love.

17

Danger Signs

Need to Know (and Believe)

- No one person can or should be "everything" to the other. So any experience or friend that helps you to grow—to become "more" you—will be valued by someone who truly cares.

- Anything less than constant respect toward you, your body, your mind, and your spirit is unacceptable.

Boundaries

Not exactly a word that conjures up love songs and sunsets. When you really like someone, you want to be together—a lot. But the point of any relationship is *not* to lose yourself. The point of any relationship you have with *any* person is to empower you to discover yourself. *To become more you.* And **boundaries—clear, no-fuss, no-drama communication of your wants, goals, fears, and limits**—are what make that kind of you-building awesomeness possible. Some are physical, some emotional, some about privacy. **Just remember: whatever you tolerate is what will continue.** That's why whatever limits one partner sets *must* be upheld by the other. Once a boundary is willfully disregarded, trust goes out the window…for good.

Healthy boundaries (like making sure you have time with your friends, family…even alone) aren't meant to keep a dating partner at arm's length. In fact, they're not about the "other" person at all. They're about maintaining a healthy sense of individuality within a relationship, about not losing "you" inside the "we." They're how to retain the sense of "self" that attracted the other person in the first place. **No one person can or should be "everything" to the other. So any experience or friend that helps you to grow—to become "more" you—will be valued by someone who truly cares.**

Of course, boundaries are always going to be unique to each person, but **in every healthy relationship, there should be no problem when/if you**:

- go out with your friends without your partner

- participate in activities and hobbies you like

- choose not to share passwords to your email, social media accounts, or phone

- appreciate, but don't always participate in, each other's individual likes and needs

- travel for work or school

- put extra time into becoming "more you" through extra study or your career.

A relationship should be an opportunity to grow together while honoring the beauty of each other's individuality.

-Lindsey Nebeker

As great as it is to want to spend a lot of time together, it really *is* important to have some time away from each other too. Ironically, those boundaries will only strengthen any relationship that's worth having. If, at any point, someone tells you that your needs are stupid, gets angry with you for speaking up, or goes against what you're comfortable with, consider this your PAY ATTENTION NOW sign. Love (even like) is respect. And *that* is *not* respectful.

"It's not like he put you in the hospital." That's what my mother said to me when I finally decided to bring criminal charges against my (finally) ex-boyfriend. Sounds harsh, right? She didn't mean it that way. She meant to protect me from public courts, from the vulnerability she knew would come from lots of people knowing some terribly personal details of my life. What she didn't understand was that I'd fought—no, I'd scratched and clawed—to find my way back to the person I'd lost in that relationship. And although my physical injuries were no more serious than grip marks on my arms or a handprint on my face, the worst injuries were the private ones of which I could barely speak. That he'd shaved his head to give me a constant visual reminder of how he hated me. That he humiliated me in deeply intimate ways I never talked about. And yet, for all of the shaming and name-calling, it wasn't until he actually struck me that I would ever have used the word "violent." I clearly remember telling another girl, "He just gets a little rough sometimes." Whatever. Anything less than constant respect toward you, your body, your mind, and your spirit is unacceptable. Completely, totally unacceptable. It's unhealthy. And often, yes, it's abuse.

We Accept the Love We Think We Deserve

Girls and women on the spectrum have a terribly great likelihood of being taken advantage of, abused, manipulated, or used. Of feeling abandoned. I've been there. The journey is subtle; after all, no one falls in love with a person who hurts, degrades, or insults her on the first date. No one expects to trade her dignity for affection. No one surrenders her sense of self without reasons…reasons that seem, in the moment, clear and right and convincing. We misunderstand jealousy and control as proof of how much we're wanted. Shapeless, self-less, we fit our words—our appearance, our behavior—to match others' ideas of love and sex. But we are nowhere to be found.

The thing is, **the all-or-nothing, now-or-never, this-person-or-all-is-lost feelings of *Romeo and Juliet* is what we're taught to expect out of love and romance**. I sure did. That's why over-the-top fallouts with boyfriends didn't scare me. In fact, they energized me a little bit. When guys got jealous, I felt powerful…

special. When I heard "You're the only one who'll ever understand me," I finally felt necessary. When he wanted to spend all of our time together, I felt loved.

This is how controlling behavior looks:

Power and Control			
Harassment	**Intimidation**	**Threats**	**Isolation**
• Follows you and often shows up uninvited. • Makes prank phone calls. • Spreads rumors. • Keeps trying to have contact after you have ended the relationship.	• Tries to scare you by smashing things, driving recklessly, yelling, or with looks/ gestures. • Threatens to get you in trouble with family, friends, or school.	• Threatens to harm you, your friends, or family. • Threatens suicide if you leave them or don't do what they want. • Threatens to break up with you.	• Pressurizes you to choose between them and your friends or family. • Pressurizes you to quit your job or other extra-curricular activities.
Sexual, Physical, Verbal, and Emotional Abuse			
Violating Your Privacy		**Limiting Independence**	**Humiliation**
• Reads your notes to or from other people. • Goes through your purse, locker, or book bag without your permission. • Forces unwanted intimacy. • Refuses to stop "wrestling" when asked.		• Wants to control what you wear and how you look. • Pressurizes you to use cigarettes, alcohol, or drugs. • Wants to make all the decisions in the relationship.	• Calls you names privately or in front of others. • Puts down or makes fun of your race, religion, class, or family. • Inappropriately grabs you or shows off your personal information in public.

This is how it happens... Again and again:

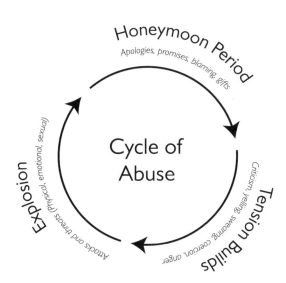

I do not want this for you. At the very least, I want no more of it for you. Until my dying day, I will also remember being in the center of a crowded college dance floor with my boyfriend. Earlier, another boy had been (unsuccessfully) flirting with me, and somehow, the same "you're so hot" quality that had attracted my boyfriend was thrown back in my face, now a dirty, ugly, shameful thing. "You may have them all fooled," he whispered in my ear. "But I know the truth. You're a bitch and a whore. Don't forget it." I don't believe him anymore, of course. But no, I haven't forgotten.

"Violence" isn't about hitting any more than eating disorders are about food. It's about taking away your control over your own mind, heart, and body…about reducing your experiences, weakening your spirit, and covering up your sparkle—instead of inspiring, supporting, and empowering the breathtaking human being you're meant to be.

But for those of us who aren't used to expecting kindness—who don't always know what "healthy" looks like—it helps to spell it out clearly. Take a look at these statements. For each, you're going to circle "O" Often, "S" Sometimes, or "N" Never.

Healthy Relationship 101: Often, Sometimes, and NEVER

In *The Asperkid's (Secret) Book of Social Rules*, I wrote:

> It's awfully hard to describe something if you haven't really seen it before. Try describing my kitchen. Unless you've been here, you have no idea if it's big or small, cozy or modern, green, yellow or gray. And if you haven't had a good friend, it's not too easy to describe that either…[which why it's so crucial that we] **define what a friend is, instead of just what s/he isn't.** (p.177)

The same is true for romantic relationships. A lot of us have seen unhealthy situations growing up. And most of us have gotten used to tolerating (or at least expecting) a certain amount of bullying in our lives. Which means there's a good chance that many folks reading this don't really have a clear picture of what "healthy" looks like. (How could they, after all?) So let's spell it out.

Section 1:

1. Is very supportive of things that I do and encourages me to try new things
   O   S   N

2. Likes to listen when I have something on my mind
   O   S   N

3. Talks to me when they're unhappy with something in the relationship
   O   S   N

4. Is willing to compromise
   O   S   N

5. Understands that we have separate interests and can spend time apart
   O   S   N

Section 2:

1. Is mean or rude to my friends
    O   S   N

2. Criticizes or distracts me when I'm doing things that don't involve them
    O   S   N

3. Gets extremely jealous or possessive
    O   S   N

4. Accuses me of flirting or cheating when I'm not
    O   S   N

5. Constantly checks up on me or makes me check in
    O   S   N

Section 3:

1. Breaks or throws things when we fight
    O   S   N

2. Threatens to destroy my things
    O   S   N

3. Tries to control what I do, who I see, what I wear, how I look or who I talk to
    O   S   N

4. Makes me feel nervous or like I'm "walking on eggshells"
    O   S   N

5. Blames me for problems, puts me down, calls me names or criticizes me
    O   S   N

Section 4:

1. Makes me feel like no one else would want me
    O   S   N

2. Threatens to hurt themselves, me, my friends, pets, or family
   O   S   N

3. Grabs, pushes, shoves, chokes, punches, slaps, holds me down, throws things, or hurts me in some other way
   O   S   N

4. Yells, screams, or humiliates me in front of other people
   O   S   N

5. Pressures, guilts, or forces me into having sex or going farther than I want
   O   S   N

How to Score

Section 1:
  For each O: subtract 5.
  For each S: subtract 3.
  For each N: do nothing.

Section 2:
  For each O: add 5.
  For each S: add 3.
  For each N: do nothing.

Section 3:
  For each O: add 10.
  For each S: add 5.
  For each N: do nothing.

Section 4:
  For each O: add 50.
  For each S: add 25.
  For each N: do nothing.

How to Interpret Your Score

Zero or "Negative" Points

Great! Your answers reflect a healthy relationship. Remember to practice your reflexive listening techniques and the other super-important get-along skills in *The Asperkid's (Secret) Book of Social Rules.*

1–5 Points

If you scored 1–5 points, you might be noticing a couple of things in your relationship that are unhealthy, but it doesn't necessarily mean they are warning signs. It's still a good idea to keep an eye out and make sure there isn't an unhealthy pattern developing.

6–10 Points

If you scored 6–10 points, it sounds like you may be seeing some warning signs and your relationship may be unhealthy. Don't ignore these red flags. Something that starts small can grow much worse over time. No relationship is perfect—it takes work! But in a healthy relationship you won't find abusive behaviors.

11–50 Points

If you scored 11–50 points, you are definitely seeing warning signs and may be in an abusive relationship.

Over 50 Points

If you scored more than 50 points, it is important to consider taking steps to ensure your safety. You don't have to deal with this alone. Please see the Resources section in the back of this book for the support you deserve. **And just so we're clear: It is absolutely, totally, and completely alright to miss people you no longer want in your life. Because one day (I promise), you will look around and think, "Remember that person I thought I couldn't live without? Well, here I am...alive...and living."**

18

The Particulars

Falling in Like with Your Eyes Wide Open

Need to Know (and Believe)

- You need the right people by your side and at your back... not necessarily the obvious people.

- You get to choose the people you want: People who will treat you well. And if you have to make new choices, it's OK. YOU will be OK. And loved. For real.

- "Dating" means different things to different people.

- Sometimes, flirting is nothing more than playful conversation between platonic friends. Sometimes, one person has romantic intentions while the other has purely physical ones. And sometimes, you may not even realize that someone is flirting with you!

- Watch people's actions and you will never be fooled by their words.

Have you ever watched people in the grocery store trying to pick out the perfect melon? Some people shake them. Others sniff them. A few knock on them. They may be "in the market," but I'm pretty sure that most of those shoppers haven't the vaguest clue how to actually find what they want.

The same can be said of Aspies and friends. We know we want friends; often, though, we don't really know how to choose good ones. In fact, you may not even realize that you should—or that you can—choose whom you befriend. When you are lonely, feel rejected or afraid, the want of companionship can feel bottomless. It's easy to compromise who we are and accept far less kindness than we deserve just to have someone by our sides. I know. I've been there. I've accepted bruises and excused them. I've been the popular one too, standing in the center of the crowd, yet feeling utterly alone.

There are so very many things I have learned about friendship and dating that I want to tell you—about levels of intimacy and trust and listening more than you speak. There is far too much to say, and it's all far too important to gloss over. So, let's cover one moment thoroughly: the one moment common to every relationship, romantic or platonic, when we actively choose who and what we will allow into our lives. Stop with me here, and realize this: You do have a choice. And you deserve to make a good one.

"The minute you settle for less than you deserve," it's been said, "you get even less than you settled for." That's true in all things, be it fruit or friends. You have to "shop" for the right relationships, too. **You need the right people by your side and at your back…not necessarily the obvious people.**

Here's what I mean: In any crowd, class, office, or club, there are naturally "attractive" people. Whether because of looks, confidence, or power, they draw others in. These "obviously attractive" folks—who may be wonderful people—already have busy social lives. They don't need to make the effort to begin yet *another* friendship.

Don't spend your energy on obvious. Don't you dare, for one more second, surround yourself with people who don't appreciate how wonderful you are. Approach people who have room for, and need of, an extra someone in their lives. That's who will most value your company and probably work hardest to deserve your affection, too.

So really, just be the kind of "someone special" you'd want to have. Be yourself. Be real. Ask questions. Listen to the answers. Ask more questions. Give compliments, don't just think them. Take turns. Smile. Notice kindnesses, and say thank you. Relationships are about balance and reciprocity in communication, in invitations, in expense (of time and money). They are about being kind more than about being right, and about glad humility—not thinking less of yourself, but thinking of yourself less.

You are not someone to have to be endured. You are not lucky to just "get" whomever walks into your life. You get to choose the people you want: people who will treat you well. And if you have to make new choices, it's OK. YOU will be OK. And loved. For real.

(Hey, Jennifer…how about some particulars?) Alright, alright. That's nice and all, but I can hear you asking for specifics. As one gal recently complained, "I can't even tell if I'm on a date or not!"

So let's start there: **What does "dating" actually mean? First, "dating" means different things to different people.** That's OK, as long as you are both clear and direct. Whomever you're with has to feel comfortable with the way you think, or you'll spend the rest of your time together trying to be someone you're not (and he or she will miss out on discovering the amazing person you actually *are*).

Next, a dating relationship may be sexual, but it does not have to be. It may be serious or casual, straight or gay, committed or open, short-term or long-term. (And yes, dating abuse can occur within all kinds of intimate relationships.)

You may also hear some of these terms used to refer to the same kinds of relationships we've just described:

- going out

- together

- being with someone

- seeing each other

- friends with benefits

- hooking up

- "talking" to.

Regardless of the words you like, just be sure that both people clearly check in as to how they see the relationship. (I'll never forget when a boy I dated during college told me he thought we ought to see other people, too…whoops! I'd never known he thought we were exclusive. I'd been dating other people all along—which, though innocent, really could've hurt his feelings.)

Who's Looking Good?

Being in the driver's seat—actively choosing who you seek out or express interest in—means you have control over who gets to enter your life and who you may want to ask to leave. (Yes, you're allowed to do that. You're *supposed* to do that! Once I'd learned how to spot "danger signs" in dating partners, I was able to end relationships sooner, *before* my heart got so wrapped up. I can still remember telling one very sweet boy, "Thanks so much for the time we've spent, but I think we've taken our relationship as far as it's going to go." Yes, he asked to stick around. I declined. And I was alone. And it was OK.)

Let me give you some really specific qualities to look for in possible boyfriends/girlfriends. Remember, of course, that no person will tick off *every* item *every* day. You're going for more yes's than no's—and NONE of the behaviors from the Power and Control Chart on p.182. The person:

- treats you with respect (pays attention to what you say, encourages you to learn and try more things)

- doesn't make fun of things you like or want to do

- doesn't insult you

- doesn't get angry if you spend time with your friends or family

- listens to your ideas, and compromises sometimes

- is more often in a good mood than in a bad one

- shares some of your interests

- isn't afraid to share their thoughts and feelings

- is comfortable around your friends and family

- is proud of your accomplishments and successes

- respects your boundaries

- doesn't require you to "check in" or need to know where you are all the time

- is caring and honest

- doesn't pressure you to do things that you don't want to do

- doesn't constantly accuse you of cheating or being unfaithful

- encourages you to do well in school or at work

- doesn't threaten you or make you feel scared

- is energized by your intelligence, not threatened by it.

A successful romantic relationship must, at its core, be a successful friendship...an equal give-and-take based on mutual respect, time, and attention. Here's what that "looks like" in real life:

- **Kindness**: friends like one another and try to make each other feel happy.

- **Perspective**: friends ask questions about each other's lives, feelings, and ideas in order to understand each other's perspectives.

- **No one loses**: true friends can disagree, argue, get mad, and solve problems together; staying friends is more important than proving who is right or wrong.

- **Things in common**: friends are never exactly alike, but they usually have a lot in common (interests, activities).

- **Slow sharing**: over time, friends gradually share ideas, wishes, and feelings that they don't share with others.

Being Bilingual

Mae West, a legendary movie siren, once said, "I speak two languages: English and body." Yeah, she sure did. Those of us on the spectrum have a much harder time "speaking" body language without purposely learning it.

Research tells us that a huge amount of communication is nonverbal, untaught, and lightning fast—universal, subtle messages that we Aspies easily miss or misinterpret. Our spectrum brains focus on things neurotypicals don't heed, and we often gloss over what others think is totally obvious. The key to what the boy you like is really thinking or whether that girl wants you to stick around is probably right in front of you, tucked into gentle hand movements and quick facial expressions. And the good news is that yes, you sure can learn to notice and give the signals you may have been missing beforehand.

"April" wanted to know how. Specifically. She asked, "How can you tell if someone likes-you-likes-you? And how do you show them without coming right out and saying it?" Well, if you want to know, too, all you have to do is crack…

The Body Language Code
Flirting

Flirting is simply another way that two people can closely interact with each other. Sometimes, flirting is nothing more than playful conversation between platonic friends. Sometimes, one person has romantic intentions while the other has purely physical ones. And sometimes, you may not even realize that someone is flirting with you!

What does flirting look like? It's a combination of things— no one sign is a reliable indicator. You're looking for several, consistent signals. **Watch people's actions and you will never be fooled by their words.**

Here are some signs to look for (or try) that say, "I'm here. I'm available. And I'm interested."
Boys often:

- stand up straighter around you (taking a wide stance)

- make a point to sit near you

- smile more than usual, and make more eye contact

- lean toward you

- "mirror" your body language (change your body position— see if he does the same!).

Girls often:

- play with their hair

- touch their face (usually lips or cheek)

- expose the neck

- lightly touch your shoulder or arm while talking with you

- "catch and away," making eye contact for one to two seconds, smiling, then looking away or down and back again.

Putting yourself "out there" is scary, sure. But you know what's even scarier? Regret.

Go where you're

CELEBRATED

NOT WHERE YOU'RE

TOLERATED.

! CAUTION

THIS does **NOT** have
the capacity to measure
Your worth.

Don't
quit your
Day
Dream

Something Special

The Evil Twins

You know how you can try to be really nice…
To say just the right thing…
And yet somehow
you still end up sounding like
    Miss Rudy Rudepants?
Yeah.
I get that.
You're good.

An old boyfriend of mine used to constantly remind me that "the road to hell is paved with good intentions." Well, yes, I suppose that very few people truly have *bad* intentions—usually, it's just a matter of perspective, of perception…and of seeing the "bigger picture." Or not. (Unfortunately, those happen to be MAJOR spectrum blind spots, which is why my good intentions so frequently seem to backfire.)

Most problems are actually caused by people's *good* intentions. Even though their motivations may not seem good (or kind or fair or wise) to *us*, they certainly seem good to the person who's taking action. You. Me. Social justice defenders. Medieval witch hunters. Modern-day bullies. **Everyone you will ever meet is afraid of something, loves something, and has lost something. That's where motivation comes from. People aren't really against anyone else. They are for themselves.** Which is why I've come to see "Intention" and "Perception" (ours and other people's) as twins—they may *look* a lot alike, but they are definitely not the same thing. One is almost "always good." The other? Well, she's not really the "evil twin." She's just very, very tricky.

However… (Insert sinister, evil-twin laugh.) Guess what I've discovered? In a few simple steps, we can actually get "her" (Perception) to work *for* us.

When:

1. You are **interacting with others** in person, online, in writing—basically, in ANY way—

2. AND you encounter an **unexpected reaction** (they get upset instead of laughing, they seem angry instead of pleased, they don't show much emotion at all to what you thought of as a big deal, etc.)…

3. STOP. You may have a "**bad perception connection.**"

4. USE this **"disconnect" as a signal** to ACT NOW. Think of it as spotty Wi-Fi or a hard-to-hear phone call. You need to **clear up the communication.**

5. Politely interrupt: "Excuse me, I'm feeling a little confused. **I think we may have a miscommunication.**"

6. ASK what the other person is *hearing* from you. **If her perception doesn't match up with your intention, say so.**

7. **Then, patiently, thank her and ask to please explain yourself again.**

And suddenly, the twins are working together.
Well done, Masterminds. Well done.

19

"Ain't I a Woman?"

Girl Power. For All.

Need to Know (and Believe)

- When girls cut one another down—name-call, exclude, or tease one another—we're doing the world's dirty work.

- "Girls" will compete with each other. "Women" empower one another.

- In the Queen Bee Court, picking someone apart—judging her clothes, her sense of humor, her intelligence, her body, her love life—is a super-common way of bonding.

- If you are burned by another woman, respond with dignity—not with more "mean girl games."

- When we participate, we perpetuate. And what we tolerate will continue.

Sojourner Truth was born a slave in 1797. Growing up, she was beaten and mistreated, like so many around her. As a young woman, she fell in love with another slave, Robert—but their master wouldn't allow the couple to wed. Instead, she was forced to marry a different man, Thomas, by whom she had thirteen children…many of whom were sold away from her care. Dehumanizing cruelty, for sure. But Sojourner fought back.

Both the antislavery *and* women's rights movements gained great strength during her lifetime, and after escaping bondage, Sojourner eventually became a nationally renowned speaker, advocate, and leader for both causes. Yet, her most famous words weren't spoken in the fight against slavery *or* on behalf of American women. What history best remembers of Sojourner Truth is a simple question: "Ain't I a woman?"

Slavery did not keep her down—other *women* did. You see, "mean girls" aren't exactly new.

In the 1800s, white American women did their sisters a great injustice. Many suffragists believed that having women of color involved in "the cause" would weaken their chances of winning the vote. Public support for women's voting rights was hard enough to come by, they argued. *Black* women's rights were an even harder sell to the nation—including to many of the white suffragettes, who had no interest in being associated with "*those*" women.

In 1851, Sojourner took the stage at the Women's Rights Convention in Ohio. Bravely, humbly, she asked them to consider whether we, women, oughtn't see ourselves as more alike than "better" or "less":

> That man over there says that women need to be helped into carriages, and lifted over ditches, and to have the best place everywhere. Nobody ever helps me into carriages, or over mud-puddles, or gives me any best place! **And ain't I a woman?** Look at me! Look at my arm! I have ploughed and planted, and gathered into barns, and no man could head me! **And ain't I a woman?** I could work as much and eat as much as a man—when I could get it—and bear the lash as well! **And ain't I a woman?** I have borne thirteen children, and seen most all sold off to slavery, and when I cried out with my mother's grief, none but Jesus heard me! **And ain't I a woman?**

Women during Sojourner's time fought as they do now—against one another, instead of for one another. Divided, they didn't gain the vote in the United States for another sixty-nine years. Instead, they wasted time and energy. They jostled to be recognized—to be heard—as if there weren't room enough in this world for *each of us* to have a voice.

Why the History Lesson?

Maybe you don't live in the U.S. Maybe you don't like history. So, why in the heck spend this time telling you about a woman who lived a long time ago and has nothing to do with *you* (at least not in any obvious way)? Simple. The rules haven't changed. While we ought to spend time building one another up, girls—of all ages—still tear each other down. And worst of all? Women and girls actually *bond* over judging one another. Over pulling each other apart. Then, we act as though it's a given. As if "girls will be girls" is an understandable explanation for being hateful. Nope. Sorry. That's an insult to *all* women. And I just won't agree to it.

Do you know how to keep any group "down"? To make sure they remain weak? It's simple, divide and conquer. Keep them fighting against one another. Distracted, convinced that there's just not "enough" (whatever) to go around, they'll spend all of their energy clawing over one another. Each one will do her best to eliminate threats—meaning no outsider has to work at it. The whole group is neutralized. They'll never have enough energy or focus to get anywhere.

That is precisely what girls do to other girls when we insult, judge, gossip about, body shame, "slut shame," or otherwise disrespect one another. When we say "skinny girls aren't real," we may *think* we're being empowering—but we're not. We're continuing the tradition of judgment. Because some *real* girls *are* skinny (and curvy, and muscular, and voluptuous, and slender). When girls cut one another down—name-call, exclude, or tease one another—we're doing the world's dirty work. We're leaving Sojourner, and you, and me out of the "clique" again. Because you see, "girls" will compete with each other—no matter if they are 16 or 56. That's immature ridiculousness. But "women" empower one another. Always. Even when it's tough. Even when others don't. Even when we don't like one another. We just don't play *that* game. Period.

But I Don't Play "Mean Girl" Games! (or Do I?): "Shaming" (of All Kinds)

Most girls don't see ourselves as sexist. But sadly, most of us would be wrong—even those of us on the spectrum, who've often been the most frequent victims of "mean girls." Call it body shaming. Call it "slut shaming." Whatever you call it, don't do it. **Because when we participate, we perpetuate. And y'all know…what we tolerate will continue. So, don't**

participate in, perpetuate, or tolerate either body shaming or "slut" shaming.

Body shaming is public criticism about another person's weight or size. If we want our worth to be measured by the "content of our character" instead of the number on a scale…if we want to be liked even on days when we have a giant pimple or our hair freaks out…we have to give at least that much to one another. Period. So when someone else loses or gains weight, don't comment. It's neither an achievement nor a tragedy. When she complains about being "bad" for eating this or that, don't reply. There's no such thing as a bad food. And no one is "bad" for indulging. Remind her—and remind yourself—that you cannot *feel* fat. You have fat (we all do). You also have toenails. You are not a toenail.

There is NO reason to see anyone's body as a constant improvement project. Remember? It's for doing, not for dissecting. So just don't go there. Even if a girl isn't popular. Or you don't really like her. Even if she isn't nice to you. Even if you love her. Even if you don't. Don't go there.

"Slut" shaming is the act of making a girl feel embarrassed for her sexuality, whether she's sexually active or not. It can take the form of direct name-calling, or it can take a more indirect approach, influencing the things girls do (or don't do) simply because they're afraid of being seen as promiscuous.

Sexual shaming creates a divide between the "slutty stupid ones" with "no self-respect" and the "proper ladies" who "deserve" to be treated as human. Instead of building women up and cultivating healthy friendships, calling each other a "ho" (for whore) or "bitch" or anything of the kind puts women into harmful categories based on nothing more than how someone dresses or is perceived by others.

As with all forms of bullying, social media has made it easier and more widespread. Now photos and texts intended for one person can be screen-grabbed and shared with the world. Rumors about hookups can spread around a school in minutes. Reputation is more slippery than ever.

Want to stop the shaming? Don't use the words. Don't insult other girls—and call out other people when they do. It's time to take control of our beautiful bodies, our lives, our sexuality…and not let other people (especially other girls!) make us ashamed of being our authentic selves.

Popularity (and Stuff)

One of my favorite songs (and there are A LOT to choose from!) from the Broadway musical, *Wicked*, is called "Popular." Bouncy and blonde, dressed in head-to-toe pink, future-"good"-witch Glinda has decided to mend her "mean girl" ways and take on a charity "project"—the transformation of her roommate, Elphaba, from "freak" to "popular girl." Elphie just has to copy Glinda, she's told, to learn "everything that really counts"—how to flirt, what slang to use, how to wear her hair. It's hard to take Glinda's over-the-top Barbie-esque personality seriously. So the song is really pretty funny…until you realize that tucked within the lyrics is an incredibly astute idea: the most powerful people in the world—heads of state, important leaders, celebrities, brilliant orators—aren't necessarily smart or wise. It's not about "aptitude," Glinda observes. It's "the way they're viewed." In other words, they're powerful because they're popular.

You might say that there are two kinds of "popular." **Some women are well liked because they make "ordinary" things and "ordinary" people feel "extraordinary."** They walk with their heads held high, with genuine smiles for all, and an attitude that others want to be around. That's attractive. And it makes for a beautiful kind of popular.

The other kind of popular isn't really about being liked at all. It's based in bullying—a social status built on fear, intimidation, and control. It's about one person building herself up by tearing everyone else down. It's not about admiration. It's not about happiness. It's about power. (Read on, sisters!)

20

Bullies, Mean Girls, and Stuff That Actually Works

Need to Know (and Believe)

- Bullying is really all about power.

- "You know how girls can be?" Yes. Girls are human beings. Therefore, they—we—can be anything, because we can FEEL everything.

- We cannot ultimately control other people's actions, words, or ideas, but we sure can influence them by having more informed, more conscious control of our own.

- There are very specific steps you can take if you're being targeted—and "just ignoring it" isn't one of them.

"When I was your age…" There's the phrase (or some version of it) that begins most adults' attempts to tell pretty much anyone younger, "I see that you're confused (or hurting or sad or lonely) and I really want you to know that you're heard, and that you matter." Only on the receiving end, it's common for even the most important I-totally-can-relate-to-that-feeling-so-know-that-you're-not-alone story to come across as if we think our experience is exactly the same as yours…so you ought to just disregard the *actual* feelings, situations, and people in your life and trust the "long ago and far away" stories we're selling. Just a guess, but I'd bet you're not buying. Even if we mean well by telling you that you're not a loser or freak or insert-insult-of-the-day-here, it's easy to see how the "advisee" doesn't feel empowered—she feels challenged. Even insulted. You're a whole lot less likely to say, "Thanks, Jennifer (or mom or whomever)…I see how all the things I'm living through are confusing and how valuable your perspective and support are" than, "Who the heck is this woman to try to tell me I don't really understand my own life? Since when did she become the expert in everything?"

So, let me try something different. Instead of assuring you (again) that you don't *actually* deserve to be abandoned, insulted, excluded, or punished (which you don't—OK, fine, I did it again), let me offer you a truth: on some level, I still fight that belief about myself daily. You can tell me otherwise, and I'll smile and agree if I'm being polite, but I may even argue and try to prove you wrong on a bad day. Because, in the end, it really doesn't matter what anyone else tells you to believe about yourself. It only matters what *you* tell yourself to believe, and then how *you* decide to make it better. If you really are feeling bad about yourself because of people problems, then you need to think through how you can feel better. Obviously, you have the smarts, the good sense, and the maturity to figure things out on your own. I am not here to argue facts with you or to try to dissect what's accurate from what's not. What's that going to accomplish? Your truth—the one that's beating in your heart right *now*—is all we need to care about. But I—and the other "storytelling" folks—*do* care and *do* have some insights that you may find helpful as you problem-solve. We're not here to preach. We're here to empathize. To walk alongside you, not to direct you. And we're asking—*I'm* asking—that for now, you trust me to brainstorm *with* you.

"You Know How Girls Can Be"

"Why do they always end up hating me?" That's a big question for a lot of us on the spectrum—who've had "eras" of friendships but never really seem to be able to keep them going over time. Either we don't know how to make friends to begin with, or we are "super-hot then super-cold." We charm everyone, only to eventually find ourselves "blown off" or downright "kicked out" in the long run. And, after enough cycles of that pattern, you can't help but ask, "What's wrong with me? Why am I so annoying to so many people?" I sure have. It's just one of the reasons I wrote *The Asperkid's (Secret) Book of Social Rules*, which started off as notes for myself—as an adult. Those "rules" are important—they're tips and tools that have made a BIG difference for a lot of people in everyday life—AND there's still more to get at. There's still the belief so many of us have that, if we're really being truthful, we deserve what we get. We earn it. Only, if we're being open and honest and admit that belief, we scare a lot of people who care about us. They see the good in us (thankfully) or the seemingly simple solutions we "inexplicably" keep missing, and they want to help. *That's* why they reply with what is essentially, "Oh, but they won't" or "Oh, you just have to do this" or "Oh, you're better off without them" or "Don't let it bother you" or "They're just jealous or insecure." Nicely meant. But not, in the end, what we need to hear or what we believe anyway.

"You know how girls can be." Heard that before? OK, world, listen up: That's not a satisfactory answer to any question. And it's *really* not helpful to *any* girl or any woman in need of *actual* guidance in the *actual* world. You want to know how to manage yourself? How to make choices that will bring about a life that matches up more closely with the one you want? You need the bravery to listen to the truth—no matter what it is. You need:

- good information

- the patience and bravery to consider what you hear

- to remember to play dominoes (because everyone else already *is* playing).

How girls can be, huh? Well, I'm a (grown-up) girl, and I'm going to tell you something: **Girls are human beings. Therefore, they—we—can be anything, because we can FEEL everything.** And what humans DO is based directly upon how they feel. So, yes, I know how girls can be. We can be brave, witty, kind, benevolent, clandestine, sneaky, creative, clever, aggressive, accepting, hopeful, cruel, uplifting, mean, exclusionary, generous…and that's just for starters! THINK. FEEL. DO. Remember the dominoes? We can and *will* be all of those things because we—like every other human being—can and will think endless thoughts…which inspire limitless emotional reactions…which result in the actions we choose to take. **Which means that although we cannot ultimately control other people's actions, words, or ideas, we sure can influence them by having more informed, more conscious control of our own. Which calls for (a) a movie, (b) bravery, and (c) strategies that actually work.**

A Movie

Watch the movie *Mean Girls*. Really. You must. Besides the fact that you'll be able to masterfully toss around pop culture must-knows like "fetch" and "grool," you'll be amazed at what the fabulous (NON-mean girls) Tina Fey and Amy Poehler manage to capture in one now-cult-classic: the ultracomplicated girl world that we are expected to navigate, survive, and move through unscathed. *That* is fiction, indeed.

In or out, us or them. The truth is that big social experiences—like whether we are included in or rejected from cliques at age five or 35—are often determined by really subtle (and really confusing) "rules." "We wear pink on Wednesdays," say the movie's "popular girls," and, "you can't sit with us if you don't." In real life, given the tantalizing chance to "belong" (sort of an oasisy Shangri-la fantasy), I'd guess that most girls *would* go find something pink to wear on Wednesday. Why? Because teasing and gossip *are* the primary weapons girls (and women) use to humiliate and undermine each other, to try to gain social power, and to set traps. And because for lots of us, there's only one thing scarier than being lonely: being targeted.

The Hive

A lot of people don't realize that "Mean Girls" is actually based on a nonfiction book, one that I mention in *The Asperkid's (Secret) Book of Social Rules* and really have to point to again. *Queen Bees and Wannabes* (by Rosalind Wiseman) explains that there are a whole lot of complicated goings-on out there in neurotypical Girl World. At the heart of everything—always—is the currency: information. That's true for men on a battlefield. It's true for women in the cafeteria. And it turns out there's an unwritten structure to the whole dynamic, one that we, on the spectrum, aren't hard-wired to work with naturally, but one of which we are, nonetheless, part.

In *Queen Bees and Wannabes* Wiseman sorts out the levels and the "roles" into which girls fall. I cannot tell you how desperately I would have loved to have read this as a young Aspergirl. Yes, I knew there were "leaders" among the girls. I can even remember one girl who literally would lean her elbow on other girls' shoulders as if they were objects, not people. It was humiliating, really. And yet, girls felt proud when she "used" them. But beyond identifying the "leader," I couldn't see any rhyme or reason. Maybe it's the same for you.

You may have heard that real bees communicate by dancing. Well, it seems that human "Queen Bees" have a routine, too, with choreographed roles and steps. The "**Queen**" uses charisma, looks, and strategy to influence the ways other girls are "allowed" to interact. **She weakens girls and their relationships so she will feel stronger and remain important to everyone.**

As Wiseman puts it (on pages 86–91), among the Queen Bee's "court" are: **sidekicks** (girls who want to take over as Queen), **floaters** (have friends in different groups), **bystanders** (want to be nice but also really want to be included), **wannabe messengers** (will do anything to be included, eventually get turned on), and **bankers** (appearing harmless to adults, they trick you into trusting them).

Cliques are complicated and confusing, subtle, and always changing. While they will never be the natural habitat of us Aspergirls, they are how most female groups work—no matter how old you are. We must learn how to find safe places and authentic friends. If we don't, we'll become "**the targets**" of neurotypical girls and, eventually, of boys, too. That's why you have to learn the structure of Queen Bees' courts, and why you deserve help handling them.

Bravery

So, now's the time for bravery. NO ONE is ever responsible for, ever asks for, or ever deserves mistreatment from another person. EVER. How another person acts toward you—even if you were (which you aren't) the single most annoying, bothersome, irritating, horrid person on the face of the earth—is ALWAYS *her* choice and *her* responsibility. And there are some things that we can do to—sometimes—influence the thinking and feeling behind others' behavior.

Fact: Usually, the "reason" another person will give to justify her anger, jealousy, annoyance, frustration, etc., is that we are "always trying to get attention" or that we "think we're better than everyone else." However accurate or inaccurate, *that's* the real reaction we often inspire in other people. So *that's* what we have to deal with.

"She Thinks She's Better Than Everyone Else"

Let's handle the last part first. *Do* you think you're better than others? Or more important? Or that different standards apply to you? I'll admit it. Sometimes I have expected the world of myself because, on some level, I felt I *was* the exception to the rule. Which meant, I guess, that I was treating everyone else like "the rule"—the not-anything-special norm. That's not intentional meanness, but it sure is arrogance. And arrogance is a sneaky little devil. It slithers in where we don't intend and communicates ideas we may not even realize.

OK, I know this part is hard—maybe scary—probably a little embarrassing. But don't worry. No one's watching. So get honest here. You've got to get brave and take a serious look in the mirror. (Just know that at one time or another, my answer to every question below has been "yes.")

- Do you cut people off a lot? Interrupt? That sends the message: What I have to say is more important than whatever you're going on about.

- Do you argue about facts when someone is trying to share her feelings? You may be concerned with accuracy, but what it says to the other person is: I think your feelings are invalid, and I'm not going to listen. I'm not arguing—I'm just explaining why I'm right.

- Are you often late? That says: My time is more important than yours.

- Do you leave messes behind where other people have to live or work? That says: *I* can't be bothered—*you* handle it. Your time is less important.

- Do you say, "Oh! That's so easy!" when others don't know an answer but you do? Switch the roles, and it wouldn't feel too good.

Here's the thing: arrogance and insecurity are two sides of the same coin. Which means that the more insecure or unsure we are, the more arrogant we're likely to be…or at least seem. It's sort of like emotional armor—we overprotect the wounded, vulnerable parts. But remember that armor is meant to deflect. And if we spend our time and energy being perfectionists who assume without listening, telling others why we're right (meaning they're wrong), who strut around trying to prove (to ourselves, in truth) how smart and attractive and worthwhile we are, what we're actually doing is screaming to the world, "Hey! Look at me! I'm seriously insecure!" in really irritating, insulting voices. And nobody wants to be around *that*. (Would *you*?)

"She's Always Trying to Get Attention"

Not long ago, in the middle of a conversation, someone said, "I love you, Jenny," to me in a tone of great warmth, sweetness, and affection. Obviously, something I'd said or done had—right then and there—inspired a bubble of good feelings to well up and pop out into the open. Something. Only, I had NO idea what that something was. So I asked, "Why do you say that—now?"

Let's be clear. If the other person hadn't known I had Asperger's or didn't know what that meant (that I'm often not thinking about or aware of the effect of my words/actions on others), I suppose my question really could have sounded self-serving. So let's translate. What I was *really* asking was, "Please tell me. What good thing am I doing right now that made you feel so good about me—because I want you to keep feeling that way, and I need to know what I should keep doing." Sure, without perspective or understanding, it might have seemed that I was seeking praise or "trying to get attention." But I wasn't. I was "reinforcement seeking."

Like a physically blind person might ask a sighted one to "paint a word picture" of what she cannot see, mind-blind people need word pictures, too. Typical people easily notice the positive or negative responses to their behavior. It's fairly effortless—as natural as actually hearing someone say "yes" or "no." Effortless to them, but not to us. Heck! Not only can't we pick up on "subtle" feedback, we don't even know we've missed anything to begin with—not until it's too late and no one is speaking to us anymore.

Except now, you have more insight, which means you have more power (and that rocks!).

Here are the facts:

- Spectrum girls need more "volume"—bolder, repeated explanations of "keep it up, here's why."

- When specifics aren't volunteered, we need to ASK for them; otherwise, we seek feedback as we might seek sensory input: Intensely. Repeatedly. Loudly.

- That reinforcement-seeking behavior *seems* like attention seeking to other people.

- They feel annoyed and irritated by it, and either push us away or move away from us.

SO…

- We HAVE to be up-front about being on the spectrum and what it means.

- We must ask for what we need: real-time explanations, examples, reinforcement of things we should keep doing… or not.

- We can recruit social/emotional "seeing-eye friends" (whom we TRUST) to volunteer that feedback.

- We must show respect for their help by accepting compliments with a gracious "thank you," AND by calmly considering their reasonable suggestions for change.

Strategies That Actually Work

In *The Asperkid's (Secret) Book of Social Rules* (p.238), I put it out there as plainly as possible:

> ...**female relationships are incredibly complicated**. So if we, as Aspergirls, are starting off at a disadvantage socially, the idea of being able to skillfully detect "frenemies" or "cattiness" is just unfair. It'd be like asking a deaf person not only to listen to music, but also to memorize the tune and start playing along. It just isn't going to happen.
>
> Imagine you were to pick up a novel you've never read. Turn to a random page, and get really close, making a telescope out of your fingers so all you could see was a single letter or maybe a word. OK, now: give me a plot summary. What? How are you supposed to tell me what happens if you can't see anything except the little spot in front of you?!
>
> Exactly. You are too close to the world of BFF's [best friends forever] and "break-ups," the sleepovers and the drama to get a good look at what's happening around you. I'm over a decade out from teenager-hood, though, and I can see better from here. So I am going to have ask you to trust me, because, sad as it is, none of this drama goes away when you turn twenty.
>
> Want my credentials before you trust me? Done. I'm an Aspergirl, like you, and I know what it's like to desperately want to fit in. I know what it is to try to get your jeans just right (but hate the feel of denim), or to think you've made a friend only to turn around and have her making fun of you right behind your back. I have starved myself to fainting, found myself in dangerous circumstances with boys I didn't trust and have let my entire idea of who I was be decided by other people.

I've also checked my brains at the door, always hopeful that what seemed too good to be true just wasn't. Always naive.

In middle school, I got "best friend" lockets with a girl I'd known less than a year. Now, I'm going to admit, I was thrilled. She was popular, and I was really proud to walk around as the other "half" of a best friend team. We'd gotten very close over the summer, and by the time school was in, we were "BFFs." We had matching outfits, sleepovers, told secrets, the whole bit. Yet within six months, another girl, who was jealous of the friendship, had convinced my friend that I was spreading rumors. She claimed I had been telling everyone I was smarter and richer and prettier (I'd said none of those things!).

Together, the two of them spent the rest of the school year plotting different ways to make me cry. For example, they arranged one particular doozy that the *entire class* knew about—except me. I was being duped into believing that a "secret admirer" was actually calling me at a sleepover party…in front of all the girls there. Well, I really should've stopped to consider the unlikeliness of the whole thing, but I suppose I was too enamored with the possibility to think clearly. The truth? The "mystery guy" was one of the boys from school disguising his voice. And yes, *everyone* knew *everything* long before I walked into school on Monday morning.

Then there were workplace rumors spread by jealous colleagues in two of my different jobs. Innocently, I'd thought that everyone would be glad to see me, a young up-and-comer, having some exciting results with my students or counseling patients. But no. They were threatened (and honestly, my excitement probably came off as arrogance). So they got mean. And they got what they wanted. I chose to leave one position out of utter misery, and in the other, found myself "conveniently" without a class to teach the following year.

Honestly, in the wake of the crazy-fast success of the Asperkids books (which is totally due to the positivity of the readers, not anything special about this author), I've met wonderful, collaborative female colleagues…and a bevy of grown women who have begun gossip-filled phone calls about me with, "I don't want to sound like a mean girl, but…"

Sigh. That's a lot like the white suffragettes who dissed Sojourner saying, "I don't want to sound racist, but…" If you have to frame your words that way, you really ought to simply keep your mouth shut. As the saying goes, "What Peter says about Paul says a lot more about Peter than it does about Paul." Or Petra. Or Pauline.

The depressing, heartbreaking reality is this: **LOTS of women and girls STILL think that they can boost their status (and their self-esteem) by bringing one another down.** It happened to Sojourner Truth. It's still happening today. Then and now, **bullying is about power—who has it, and who doesn't**.

That, my friends, is why you have some thinking to do. In life, you're going to be left out, talked about, lied to, and used. So, **YOU have to decide who is worth your tears and who isn't. And when you are burned by another woman, will you respond in kind or will you set boundaries for yourself without playing the "mean girl" games?**

Why the Meanness?

Kids taunt other kids out of a need to belong. So do teens. So do adults. Just ask anyone who's *ever* said *anything* "behind someone's back" or made fun of someone else (even of a parent) to get a laugh. The awful truth is that hurting or excluding others is often a way to show "loyalty" to "us," not "them."

Worse yet, in the Queen Bee Court, picking someone apart—judging her clothes, her sense of humor, her intelligence, her body, her love life—is a super-common way of bonding. Of connecting. It's almost like another unwritten, horrible social rule: When girls can't think of anything to say, the trick is to talk badly about someone who isn't there. To share something you've overheard. To "worry about her"—which is code for "form a little jury and pass judgment on her."

Well, guess what? Anyone who gossips *with* you will gossip *about* you. When we get that sinking feeling, wondering if those same "friends" we've been giggling with talk like that when we're not there...the answer is yes.

At its core, bullying is how one person attempts to gain or reinforce power and control. It's the DO, which means it comes *after* a thought and a feeling. **And while we can't control how others feel about themselves, we can consider whether something we are saying or doing might be affecting/ triggering her feelings. Which means we have more power than we think.**

For example, **a "mean girl" may**:

- **be jealous** (of a friendship, looks, smarts, money, male attention, success)

- **be in need of attention**, which usually means genuine validation of her own worth

- **be angry** (perhaps about how she's been treated previously or is being treated presently at home)

- **be afraid** (of losing social status, being unwanted, having to face her own insecurities)

- **feel threatened** (just because you are witty, beautiful, talented, intelligent, etc., doesn't mean she's not, but a lot of women need reminding that there's more than enough approval to go around).

Remember to play dominoes! If she's feeling one of those feelings, what thoughts might have come first? Is there an action you could take that would cause different thoughts...then feelings...then actions on her part?

How to Spot a "Mean Girl Kind of Bully" (and Why They Do What They Do)

Your best protection against bullying is good information. Let's start with a second Power and Control Chart (because once again, the issue really is power and control):

Bullying, Power, and Control			
Humiliation	**Threats and Intimidation**	**Emotional Abuse**	**Minimising, Denying, and Blaming**
• Calling you names privately or in front of others. • Putting down or making fun of your race, religion, class, or family. • Showing off your personal items in public.	• Threatening future physical harm. • Making you do illegal things. • Making you change your story. • Tries to scare you with looks/actions. • Damaging property. • Threatening to get you in trouble.	• Putting you down and making you feel bad about yourself. • Using mocking nicknames. • Staring, giggling, and laughing at you. • Saying certain words that trigger a reaction from a past event.	• Saying you started it. • Shifting responsibility for behavior.
Sexual, Physical, Verbal, and Emotional Violence			
Social Isolation	**Social Status**	**Technology**	**Economic Abuse**
• Spreading rumours and gossiping. • Refusing to socialize with you. • "Silent treatment." • Condemning others who wish to socialize with you. • Publicly criticizing your manner of dress and other socially significant markers.	• Treating you like a servant. • Using you to inflict abuse on others. • Controlling your involvement in school and/or social activities.	• Sending and/or spreading nasty messages via cell phones, social media, Email, etc. • Spreading private information or tricking you into telling them things. • Pretending to be someone else and posting things to damage your reputation.	• Demanding money. • Stealing money and/or possessions. • Accusing you of stealing or damaging property to get them in trouble. • Jeopardizing employment due to harassment.

I want you to be able to identify "mean girl" behavior as soon as possible so you can take care of yourself better and sooner. **Notice I'm saying mean girl behavior. That's because I am not about to label any person as "mean"—our issue is with her choices.** Here's what to look for. **Bullies:**

- Talk about themselves. A lot. They cut you off to talk about their…well, anything.

- Make up "rules" that determine who's in and who's left out. You'll also see them use intimidation, threats, put-downs, and sweet-to-your-face-but-behind-your-back insults.

- Look for victims who are loners and outcasts, afraid to fight back, too shy to stick up for themselves. They choose girls who don't have allies to defend them. In other words, they pick girls who are just like a lot of us.

- Often slam other girls who stand out because of their looks (either as "too pretty" which feels threatening or "too ugly" who seem like easy targets).

- Pit friends against each other, making the others insecure and lonely—and making the mean girls seem even more important to everyone.

- Are unpredictable and manipulative.

- Don't *usually* beat up other girls physically; their weapons of choice tend to be **exclusion (leaving someone out on purpose), hurtful words, lies, vicious gossip, and whispered seeds of doubt**. ("I don't want to seem ugly, but…" followed by just enough poison to imply something that no one else had even considered. Suddenly everyone sees a damaged version of you they'd never even considered before.)

- Initially see other girls as potential competition. They scan you up and down, assessing your body language and appearance in a way that says, "I'm judging you."

- Gives a "fake smile." (Look for an expression where her mouth turns upwards, but her eyes don't crinkle happily—that crinkle shows more sincere goodwill.)

- Wants to make every other girl look bad so that nobody will see the mean girls' deep rooted insecurities.

- Says "we all" and "all of us" and "everyone thinks or knows or says" as power plays. Those phrases make one person's opinion sound like the results of some huge, unanimous vote. (Often, the mean girl doesn't even speak for the *real* feelings of other girls in her own clique.)

What to Do if You Are Being Targeted

If you find yourself being hurt, upset, or harassed by anyone, you have two main options (notice that "just ignore it" isn't one of them):

- You can confront her.

- You can ask an authority figure for help.

In either case, here's how to clear away some of the drama and get your thinking to be more effective:

1. **Make a list of specific events/incidents, and the dates, people, and places involved. Steer clear of adjectives. Just record facts—they'll speak for themselves, especially when grouped (you're establishing a pattern here).** If we add descriptors, it's easy for others to feel as if we don't trust *their* ability to respond appropriately. And *that's* certainly not going to work in our favor.

2. Add two items to each point: how you felt in response to each incident, and what you said or did.

3. Write out EXACTLY what you want to happen that will stop the behavior.

Very few people actually enjoy conflict. It's uncomfortable. Awkward. Generally icky. AND it's also inevitable. Even Gandhi, Martin Luther King, and Mother Teresa knew it. Conflict (properly handled) is a necessary part of ensuring personal respect, human dignity, and peace. That's true on a global scale *and* in the hallways of every school or office in the world. **What makes all the difference between conflicts, drama, and bullying is the goal you have in mind: addressing the situation or disagreement in a way that treats yourself and everyone else involved with dignity. (You don't have to like them, you just have to like yourself after dealing with them.) You need to speak your truth, to bravely stand up and face the situation, without turning over control (which will leave you feeling sad and lame, or even worse, regretful or embarrassed for even trying to handle the problem).**
How you do it:

- Let's start by reframing the concept of "asking for help." Never be too afraid or too proud to ask for the benefit of someone else's wisdom. Whether you choose a parent, a teacher, a counselor, your boss, an advisor, etc., one of the most important skills you are ever going to develop is asking *the right person* (not any person or every person or *no* person) for help. It's a mature decision which shows the desire for more control—more agency—over your life. And that's *all good.*

- Let's say you've decided to speak directly to the other person. **The first thing you need to do—always—is consider the "stage," that is, where and when this conversation is going to happen.** If you have an audience, she's going to feel pressured to save face, to appear justified, and is a lot less likely to listen to anything you say. If it's in writing (i.e. email, text) it can be forwarded to anyone, anywhere…it can be altered, edited, and commented on. DO NOT go this route. Just don't. It's an invitation to revictimization.

- **Prepare: Even if you don't like the other person, be smart. Give real time and thought to the other person's perspectives, regardless of the fact that you don't agree.**

- **Remember the goal: Be clear, calm, and specific about whatever you don't like. What do you want to happen next? Spell it out.**

- **Say it aloud: I have every right to be here and to be treated with dignity. So do you. I'm willing to listen and even to own anything I could have done differently, but I'm not willing to be treated with disrespect.**

- **Establish what's next: Set whatever boundaries you need in order to feel safe and happy. If you'd like to heal a wounded friendship, say so. If you'd like to end contact here and now, say so. If you'd like to suggest a cooling-off period and a follow-up conversation, set a date and take that break.**

Quiet dignity always speaks louder than screaming insecurity. So, remember to stand straight, keep your voice steady (not shrill or mumbly), and look the other person in the eye (or the "third eye"—that space between her eyebrows). This is how you communicate your personhood—your not-desperate-and-not-aggressive calm that says "I am here, too. Deal."

In response to you, **she will be**:

- genuinely surprised and/or apologetic at how she's made you feel...OR...

- uncomfortable at your bravery—don't be surprised if she tries to brush you off or (my personal favorite—ick!) say that you're "being hypersensitive" or "overreacting." That's just an attempt to clear her own conscience, which has nothing to do with you...OR...

- rude and mean…still. **That's when you go to an adult (a teacher, school counselor, psychologist, parent, etc.) for support.** They will *not* think less of you because you're being treated badly, but if the first person you talk with doesn't come up with an action plan, try someone else.

What Else Can You Do?

- If you do ask someone to speak for you (an authority figure, parent, teacher, friend, etc.), be explicit about what you want to happen. Don't assume they'll understand.

- "Can't you take a joke?" Yes, you can. And that is the single oldest method in the world of making someone doubt herself. Laughs don't have to come at the expense of someone else. So, yes, take a joke but don't take the bait. If you're getting hurt, it's not funny. And you don't have to laugh.

- Don't engage when you're upset. Breathe. Get a cold drink. Buy yourself a little time to plan your actions.

- Try to **think about why the other girl is feeling triggered** by you (see the list above). Remember that she's acting based on her own feelings, which are based on her own thoughts. If you can figure out what negative thoughts might be going on inside her head (for example, "She thinks she's so much smarter than me,") you can try to "play dominoes backwards" and counter those ideas.

- If you want help, but **want to keep your request anonymous**, call or leave a note in the school/work office with a message that says: "Hi, I'd like to keep my name private, but I wanted to let you know that _____ is being harassed by _____. Could you please tell the principal to keep an eye out?" This way no one knows you're calling about yourself or a friend of yours.

- Choose an extracurricular activity where you're likely to meet other people with similar interests. **You'll automatically feel more confident, as you'll feel less alone.**

Because you are *not* alone. We are different. Together. And this story is just beginning.

Different is neither better nor worse – just different, and different can be extraordinary.

~ Haley Moss

Need to Know (and Believe) Bulletpoint Recap

- Being extraordinary is what creates value.

- "Normal" is a role played by many but lived by none.

- Lovability has nothing to do with anyone else...with whether they seek you or leave you.

- Good people reflect and magnify who you are, but lasting confidence (and contentedness) only grows from the inside out.

- You can't expect anyone else to do *for* you what you aren't willing to do for *yourself.*

- We often mistake our most immeasurable gifts for shameful flaws.

- You are lovable. Right now. Without changing a single thing.

- In fiction, "spoilers" ruin everything. In real life, they *are* everything.

- Listening to someone does not mean that you accept their version of truth. It just means you have the confidence and courtesy to let them finish.

- Comparison is the greatest thief of joy.

- You can't be excited to grow up and also believe—on any level—that women have an "expiration date."

- Learn from those who start out before you. Teach those who come afterwards.

- Knowing yourself takes effort and courage. And LOTS of time.

- Your driving forces are those which need the most energy. Give them your time and attention, and life will feel better right away.

- We tend to think in a bottom-up style, starting with specific, concrete experiences, facts, and examples. Then, we spot trends, notice patterns, and discover the bigger concepts that link it all together.

- Every day, in many ways, you choose the life you live. We all do.

- You have to know where you're going in order to plan how to get there from here.

- Goals can (and should) change as you grow—as you go. But, if you don't even know where the target is, you can't aim your energy, time, or money in the right direction. Really, you can't aim it in any direction at all.

- Plan for any goal the same way: Envision where you want to end up. Remember that life operates in a "DO–THINK–FEEL" cycle.

- You are powerful.

- We are in charge of the choices we make and the consequences of those choices.

- Sad is a mood. It's real, it's hard, but it's temporary. And you *can* do hard things.

- You are the heroine in your own life story. Act. Don't be acted upon.

- Sometimes, painful experiences are the only way to learn the lessons we didn't even realize we needed to know.

- "No" is a complete sentence. It doesn't require apology or explanation.

- There are usually ways that you can stick to your beliefs without offending others.

- Recognize. Reply. Recommend. Or use a code word.

- Sometimes, the scariest, saddest decisions are the very best you'll ever make.

- Everything about fear is primal. There's no logic involved.

- If we focus all of our energy on curbing tantrums or meltdowns without addressing the cause of our anxiety, nothing will change.

- Every person on the HUMAN spectrum must LEARN to:

  ° RECOGNIZE her needs

  ° TALK to herself

  ° ASK FOR what she needs

  ° IDENTIFY AND CHOOSE a solution

  ° ACCESS that solution independently.

- When we are keyed up emotionally—maybe angry or frustrated, nervous, worried, even giddy or excited—we are much more likely to do and say things impulsively.

- Planning is power.

- Notepads are a great way to "let it out" without actually letting it out.

- Always remember HALT (hungry, angry, lonely, tired).

- Other people don't like you more if, by expecting more of yourself, you make them feel less.

- Whomever you're worried about impressing isn't paying all that much attention to what you do or don't do flawlessly. They're thinking about themselves.

- Perfectionism is the highest form of self-harm. You'll *never* feel perfect, but you will always feel like a failure.

- You are not a done deal.

- On those days when you truly can't say anything nice about yourself—practice.

- You are not empty or blank. You are a person with power, rights, and wants, even if you're not yet sure what they are.

- Pleasure is not a dirty word.

- Sexuality is a mix of emotional closeness, sensuality, gender and orientation, reproduction and health, active expression, freedom, and power.

- Even when you try to listen to and figure out your deepest self, it can be really hard to tell which inner voice is your own.

- Some spectrum girls aren't interested in "classically girlie" things. Others are very interested. Both are completely fine. How you "do female" is yours to invent, change, rework, and be proud of, without explanation to anyone else.

- "Hot" and "beautiful" are not the same thing. Neither are "want" and "like."

- When you are up "on a pedestal," you can get knocked down fast. No one looks you in the eye as an equal when you're up there. They look at you as an object. And every object is disposable.

- Your body was designed for YOU to understand, control, and enjoy.

- Trusting a search engine to give you the right information is like hitchhiking and expecting to get home safely. Not smart.

- There is nothing bad or shameful or sinful about the very parts which make us female.

- Whatever your particular figure, your body is brilliant and useful.

- Private parts (those covered by bathing suits) should only be discussed and/or touched in private places (rooms with doors) by yourself, a doctor, or an intimate partner.

- No matter your age, religion, culture, or nationality, YOU have complete, inarguable ownership of your body.

- Your body is not a prize to be won, a currency to trade for kindness, or an object to be bought through time, effort, or gifts.

- Most things that sound as if they're about looks or body image really aren't—they're about feeling wanted, approved of, worthwhile. Or about not feeling any of those things.

- A well-meant compliment deserves gracious acceptance.

- How you handle compliments gives a public glimpse of your self-worth and clear instructions on how the world should treat you.

- Learn the "Five Steps to Compliment Comfort"—an easy system to help consider both the strengths others notice and any constructive feedback they offer, too.

- When we don't see ourselves reflected back (truthfully) anywhere in what's supposed to be "our culture" (mainstream or spectrum), we are reduced everywhere.

- A scale just shows your numerical relationship to gravity! It doesn't measure talent, beauty, possibility, strength, or love.

- Your body wasn't created to be observed. It exists to do.

- Lingerie (bras and panties) should feel comfortable and beautiful to you, protect your modesty, and allow you to move as you'd like. Your underwear has nothing to do with pleasing anyone else.

- When you love someone, the idea of living without him or her may be heartbreaking and sad, but it does not mean the world is over.

- The all-or-nothing, now-or-never, this-person-or-all-is-lost feelings of *Romeo and Juliet* is what we're taught to expect out of love and romance.

- "Violence" isn't about hitting any more than eating disorders are about food. It's about taking away your control over your own mind, heart, and body.

- Self-advocacy is teaching other people to treat us with dignity and respect. It is asking for what we deserve, and not accepting anything less.

- No one person can or should be "everything" to the other. So any experience or friend that helps you to grow—to become "more" you—will be valued by someone who truly cares.

- Anything less than constant respect toward you, your body, your mind, and your spirit is unacceptable.

- You need the right people by your side and at your back... not necessarily the obvious people.

- You get to choose the people you want: people who will treat you well. And if you have to make new choices, it's OK. YOU will be OK. And loved. For real.

- "Dating" means different things to different people.

- Sometimes, flirting is nothing more than playful conversation between platonic friends. Sometimes, one person has romantic intentions while the other has purely physical ones. And sometimes, you may not even realize that someone is flirting with you!

- Watch people's actions and you will never be fooled by their words.

- When girls cut one another down—name-call, exclude, or tease one another—we're doing the world's dirty work.

- "Girls" compete with each other. "Women" empower one another.

- In the Queen Bee Court, picking someone apart—judging her clothes, her sense of humor, her intelligence, her body, her love life—is a super-common way of bonding.

- When you are burned by another woman, will you respond in kind or will you set boundaries for yourself without playing the "mean girl" games?

- When we participate, we perpetuate. And what we tolerate will continue.

- Bullying is really all about power.

- "You know how girls can be?" Yes. Girls are human beings. Therefore, they—we—can be anything, because we can FEEL everything.

- We cannot ultimately control other people's actions, words, or ideas, but we sure can influence them by having more informed, more conscious control of our own.

- There are very specific steps you can take if you're being targeted—and "just ignoring it" isn't one of them.

Your Song

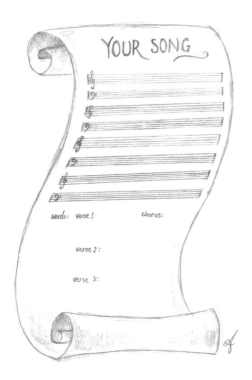

On the day you were born
    something changed.
In all the time that had ever been
Never had there been a moment
    that contained
You.
Then…suddenly…you contained a moment.
An hour.
A day.
A year.

Now, you contain so much more.
Now, you contain all that we,
Your Sisters on the Spectrum,
Have gifted you.
You have all of our love and experiments
    and laughter and tears
    and our years of knowledge and wisdom
    and curiosity.
And our friendship.
And now…
The microphone is yours.
So consider and question
And doubt and grow
And test and try and stretch
And laugh and dance
And ask.
This wacky, quirky, wild life
    doesn't go as planned, and that's OK.
Because you've got this.
And we've got you.
And you are strangely,
    wondrously,
    secretly,
    urgently,
    chaotically amazing.

Now…

When I lean in close to you

…there's music where there was silence.
There's opinion and creation and voice…and
    courage.
And beauty all your own.
There are new thoughts. New ideas. New lyrics.
A new melody alongside ours.
Because in your own voice
    in your own time,

You've begun to sing.
And it's your voice we hear,
    not our echo.
Raise your voice,
Mighty Beauty,
And sing.
Sing in cracked notes and perfect pitch.
Open the music in your wondrous, wonderful heart.
We will be here…always
    to lead you…to accompany you.
We will applaud you and teach you
And you…
You will be a masterpiece.

Resources

Please Trust Them. Please Use Them.

Study the Classics. Write Your Own Rules.

Whatever you learn about—literature, fashion, music—always start with the classics. Find out what makes them lasting favorites. Then you'll know what you like, what you don't, and you'll be ready to add your own special flair. So, first I've GOT to invite you to visit/read:

www.Asperkids.com/girl-talk

www.pinterest.com/Asperkids/spectrum-chicks-geek-girls

Cook O'Toole, J. (2013) *The Asperkid's Book of (Secret) Social Rules.* London: Jessica Kingsley Publishers.

OK, it's other folks' turn. Here are some of my favorite primers in:

Books

Ashton, J. (2009) *The Body Scoop for Girls: A Straight-Talk Guide to a Healthy, Beautiful You.* New York: Avery.
A no-holds-barred guidebook written by a fabulous, funny doctor that'll help cut through the embarrassment you may feel about your own body and arm you with the knowledge you need to make smart choices.

Schaefer, V. (2012) *The Care and Keeping of You: The Body Book for Younger Girls, Revised Edition.* Middleton, WI: American Girl.

Natterson, C. (2013) *The Care and Keeping of You 2: The Body Book for Older Girls.* Middleton, WI: American Girl.

The head to toe guides.

Conrad, L. and Loehnen, E. (2012) *Lauren Conrad Beauty*. New York: HarperCollins.
Tips for everyday make-up techniques and tricks of the trade for special-occasion looks.

Drill, E., McDonald, H. and Odes, R. (2002) *The Looks Book*. New York: Penguin.
Everything from nose jobs to breast size to pubic hair gets the smart-but-funny treatment. Learn about the history, culture, science, and business of beauty, while having fun with your looks.

Gunn, T. and Maloney, K. (2007) *Tim Gunn: A Guide to Quality, Taste & Style*. New York: Abhrams.
Every aspect of creating and maintaining your personal style— how to dress for various occasions, how to shop everywhere from designer to chain to vintage stores, how to pick a fashion mentor, find the perfect fit, and more.

Wiseman, R. (2009) *Queen Bees and Wannabes: Helping Your Daughter Survive Cliques, Gossip, Boyfriends, and the New Realities of Girl World*. New York: Three Rivers Press.
Rosalind Wiseman's classic simply rocks. It's written for parents, but I KNOW you'll want to read this treasure trove for yourself.

Online
Beauty Redefined
www.beautyredefined.net
Tools to empower girls and women as they recognize and reject harmful messages about their bodies and what "beauty" means and looks like. Beauty Redefined is all about rethinking our ideas of "beautiful" and "healthy."

ReachOut
http://us.reachout.com

An information and support service that uses evidence-based principles and technology to help teens and young adults who are facing tough times and struggling with mental health issues. All content is written by teens and young adults *for* teens and young adults, to meet them where they are and help them recognize their own strengths in order to overcome their difficulties and/or seek help, if necessary.

Sex, Etc.

http://sexetc.org

This site is on a mission to improve teen sexual health through honest and accurate information. They help teens with answers to their question about sex, relationships, pregnancy, sexually transmitted diseases, birth control, sexual orientation, and more.

Love Is Respect

www.loveisrespect.org

Loveisrespect is a project of the National Domestic Violence Hotline and Break the Cycle. By combining resources and capacity, they are reaching more people, building more healthy relationships and saving more lives.

Loveisrespect.org was designed to:

- Create the ultimate resource for fostering healthy dating attitudes and relationships.

- Provide a safe space for young people to access information and get help in an environment that is designed specifically for them.

- Ensure confidentiality and trust so young people feel safe and supported—online and off.

loveisrespect.org is the ultimate resource to engage, educate and empower youth and young adults to prevent and end abusive relationships.

Though LoveIsRespect is based in the U.S., they offer around-the-clock, completely free and confidential online chats with trained peer counselors. The live chat (IM-style) on loveisrespect.org is one way to contact a peer advocate. No relationship question is off limits, too crazy or embarrassing. They are here to help.

AND…You can also visit *www.hotpeachpages.net* for a list of vetted resources around the world.

General Awesomeness
Amy Poehler's Smart Girls at the Party
www.AmySmartGirls.com

A hub for teens, parents, teachers, and fans of all ages to learn, to become a part of the greater Smart Girls community, and to participate in Smart Girls projects. The website has grown and evolved toward online campaigns to engage followers in volunteerism, civic activism, cultural exchange, and self-expression through the arts. (And Amy's YouTube "Ask Amy" series for tween/teen girls is one of the *best* things on the Internet.)

Discover the Work of our "Yellow Brick" Sisters Online

Rudy Simone: *www.help4aspergers.com*

Sarah E. Vaughn: *www.fineartbyvaughn.com*

Temple Grandin: *www.templegrandin.com*

Haley Moss: *haleymossart.com*

Brigid Rankowski: *www.aroadtome.blogspot.com*

Helen Wallace-Iles: *www.autism-all-stars.org*

Chloe Rothschild: *www.facebook.com/pages/Chloe-Rothschild*

Robyn Steward: *www.robynsteward.com*

Zaffy Simone: *www.facebook.com/AWETISM*

Anne-Louise Richards: *www.facebook.com/AnneLouiseRichards*

Karen Kreycha: *www.autismempowerment.org*

Lindsey Nebeker: *nakedbrainink.com/lets-get-personal*